QUEER SIGNALS HEARD.

Norfolk Men Think They May Have Come From Mars.

NORFOLK, Va., August 23.—Queer radio signals were picked up here yesterday. As to whether they had any connection with the visit of the planet Mars or were merely a coincidence, local wireless experts would not venture an opinion.

Just before 1 o'clock and shortly after Government sending stations had broadcast orders to all naval receiving stations to be on the alert for any possible Martian messages, B. A. Mabry and B. G. Cowan, in charge of the powerful receiving set in the office of the chief dispatcher of the Atlantic Coast Line Railway, picked up a message unlike anything they had ever heard.

The message was not in any known code and the tone was declared as "distant and warbling, like a faraway train whistle." As near as they could make out, the radio men said, the signals corresponded to WF in the Universal code, but was composed of a queer mixture of dots and dashes. It continued for about 15 minutes.

The railway set, one of the most powerful in this section, was tuned in at 2,300 meters. Both Mabry and Cowan are veteran operators.

Photograph of UFO c. 1927

UFOS IN THE ROARING TWENTIES

AMERICAN SIGHTINGS

1920-1929

By Noe Torres & John LeMay

ROSWELL BOOKS.COM

Roswell, New Mexico · Edinburg, Texas

Cover Illustration by Jolyon Yates

Torres, Noe.
LeMay, John.
    UFOs in the Roaring Twenties:
    American Sightings (1920-1929)
        1.   History—1920s. 2. Ufology—Study of
            Unidentified Flying Objects. 3. Folklore, early
            day America.

Noe Torres: In Memory of Elizabeth Young and Penny McLeaish, two amazing teachers that shaped my love of culture and literature.

John LeMay: For Amy McVay Tellez, who I have a feeling would have been right at home in the fashions of the 1920s.

ACKNOWLEDGMENTS

This book, and the others in this series, would never have been written without the encouragement and support of a long list of dear friends, not the least of which is Ruben J. Uriarte, fellow traveler on our amazing interstellar flight.

PREFACE

THE SO-CALLED "ROARING Twenties" were christened such for good reason. A lot was going on. America had fought in and won the first World War in the prior decade. Women had won the right to vote. Penicillin was created along with other advancements in the field of medicine. Technology was growing once again in leaps and bounds. Entertainment in particular exploded in the form of movies and radio. While automobiles and household phones had been luxuries in the bygone Victorian Age, now they were becoming more common place (primitive though they may still be). The concept of man flying through the air in planes was no longer as far out as it once had been. Charles Lindbergh became famous when he conducted the first solo nonstop transatlantic flight in 1927 in his plane the *Spirit of St. Louis.* "Strange things" in the sky were no longer quite so strange. Except for when they were. With man taking to the skies in biplanes came the first sightings of UFOs while persons were in the air.

The 1920s also had several fascinating UFO cases that managed to encompass well known facets of the era. We were shocked to find that a sighting of a USO had ties to the bootlegging industry. The Prohibition Act went into effect on January 17, 1920, to the dismay of many people across the U.S. It wouldn't be repealed until the early 1930s. Mobsters and other persons involved in organized crime took advantage of the situation by the smuggling and bootlegging of liquor. One of the main figureheads of this effort was Al Capone. Speaking of Capone; the mob itself was one of the only aspects of the 1920s that we couldn't tie to UFOs (but darned if we didn't try to find something!)

Then there was the great spiritualist movement with a bizarre interest in the occult that wouldn't resurge again until the 1970s. A famous poet who liked to give lectures while dressed like a druid also sighted a UFO. Her companions, due to their spiritualist beliefs, thought that the craft came from a parallel dimension rather than outer space. They called this dimension Etheria and even claimed the U.S. government knew all about it.

As you can see, even people back in the 1920s believed that the government knew more about the mysterious "airships" than they let on. In fact, the year 1924 even sported what could be the first cover-up of a UFO crash by the Men in Black. As you will soon discover, there really is nothing new under the sun when it comes to UFO lore...

CONTENTS

1

THE MINI UFO

Mount Pleasant, Iowa
June 3, 1920

ON JUNE 3, 1920, ON HIS 22nd birthday, Jesse Clark Linch of Mount Pleasant, Iowa, observed a strange, diminutive UFO and watched it land within 15 feet of where he sat fishing. The sighting was significant enough to be included in Jerome Clark's *The UFO Encyclopedia: The Phenomenon from the Beginning,* 3rd edition (2018).

The incident occurred near a pond just outside of town, where Linch was fishing on this summer day. While sitting at the edge of the pond, Linch noticed movement over the top of a nearby grove of 100-foot-tall maple trees.

Flying over the top of the trees was a sort of disc-shaped object that was predominantly blue in color. Its size was "like a five-gallon cream can," said the witness. The size and shape have led some researchers to describe it as a "Mini UFO."

Antique 5-Gallon Cream Can

The UFO zoomed out from behind the grove of trees without making a sound. As Linch watched in amazement, the strange blue craft swooped across the pond toward where he was sitting. It hovered over the ground nearby and finally effected a landing at a spot about 15 feet away from him.

As he continued to observe the landed object, Linch was not inclined to make any sudden moves.

"I wasn't in any hurry to jump up and run over to it, and I'm glad I didn't. It might have killed me. Just when I thought about going over to take a closer look at it, it took off without any sound and without turning around."

"[It] slowly lifted over the trees in the west and disappeared – still no noise," Linch said. The object departed at a very slow speed, according to Linch, who said it traveled at a speed of "probably about four or five miles per hour." After the object's departure, he found indentions in the grass where it had lain, but there were no burn marks or other damage.

Linch kept the story to himself, because, as he said, "You didn't talk about flying saucers in those days."

Could this small UFO have actually been some type of alien probe or drone? In other books in this series, we have written about bizarre drone-like flying devices that have been seen as far back as the 1800s. Highly advanced drones such as this are widely available today were not developed until 2006.

This 1920 incident was eerily similar to a case that occurred 42 years earlier, in February 1878, at Osceola Township, Iowa, as covered in our book *The Real Cowboys & Aliens: Old West UFOs, 1865-1895.* In the Iowa case, the object was "about the size of a half bushel," which is roughly similar in size to the 1920 object. The Iowa UFO had an intensely bright light on it, such that when witnesses first spotted it they thought "the light proceeded from a lantern, carried by someone traveling the highway."

Strange Phenomenon.

A few days ago we were told a strange story in relation to an incident said to have occurred in Osceola tp., one evening last week. A young man well known in the community and regarded of undoubted veracity, relates that he was going home across the fields from a neighbor's when his attention was attracted by a light moving along the road at some distance from him. He thought at first that the light proceeded from a lantern, carried by some one traveling the highway, but as it approached nearer he noticed that it was much larger than a lantern. When the light reached a point in the road nearly opposite him it stopped and came directly toward him with great velocity, until it was within a few feet of him when it stopped. The observer describes it as about the size of a half bushel and of intense brightness. It then rose in the air a distance of several rods and then began to descend where the gentleman stood. He says that he is not usually easily frightened, but he could not account for the strange sight and he retraced his steps to the house he had just left. The light followed him until he reached the house when it went off a short distance and he lost sight of it. He told the people what he had seen and asked a couple of young men who were there to accompany him home. They started, but could see nothing of the phenomenon described, for a few moments, when it again made its appearance and was distinctly seen by all three. It did not come so close as before but would suddenly disappear and soon come in sight again in an entirely different direction and at a considerable distance from where it was last seen. The light was also seen by the people at a number of houses in the neighborhood. None of those who were witnesses of the strange occurrence are able to give any explanation of the phenomenon. That they are all honest in the recital of what they saw is conceeded by all who know the parties. We venture no explanation.—*Hampton Chronicle.*

Ackley (Iowa) Enterprise, 2-8-1878, p. 1

Researchers have speculated that these seemingly remote-controlled, unmanned aircraft are some type of surveillance drones sent out from larger UFOs. While their appearance caused wonder and speculation among eyewitnesses, the impact was a lot less than if the witnesses had seen a large alien spacecraft with its humanoid occupants.

The witness to the 1920 sighting, Jesse Clark Linch, passed away on July 26, 1977, at the age of 79, and unfortunately, his sighting remains unsolved to this day.

2

LINCOLN LAPAZ AND THE "MONSTER METEOR"

Near Okmulgee, Oklahoma
June 8, 1920

ON JUNE 8, 1920, HUNDREDS of witnesses in several states saw an intensely bright object streak across the sky from west to east. The object resembled a "falling airplane," according to a noted astronomer of the time, Lincoln LaPaz. "The professor stated that the meteor was a bright blue color until it exploded, when it burst into leaping flames of red, like an airplane afire, as it dashed downward from the heavens," according to the *Winfield (Kansas) Daily Courier.*

NASA Illustration of Meteor Strike

The amazing spectacle was witnessed by persons in Missouri, Kansas, Oklahoma, and Arkansas. One newspaper account stated that when it passed over Tulsa, Oklahoma, it appeared to be "within a few hundred yards of the earth and that the lower and heavier portion was of a greenish blue color, followed by a long wedge-shaped tail."

According to researcher Jerome Clark, there were reports of the object making a sharp right turn to the east over the town of Rushville, Missouri, after which it vanished into the clouds about two miles outside of town. At one point in its trajectory, it descended to within 75 feet of the ground.

In Bartlesville, Oklahoma, witnesses said the object lit up the city with a brilliant bluish color for about 30 seconds, which testified to the intensity of light from the object as it traversed the night sky.

AS AIRPLANE FALLS

GREAT METEOR CAME DOWN IN FLAMES

Many Winfield People Observed Brilliant Phenomenon In Southeast Tuesday Evening

"It looked like an airplane falling in flames," is the way one citizen described the brilliantly luminous phenomenon which appeared for a brief time in the southeastern sky about nine o'clock Tuesday night. Other citizens report having seen the meteor and hearing its hissing sound as it descended.

From the morning papers it transpires that the meteor fell near Okmulgee, and that it was seen as far away as Wichita. Its resemblance to a falling airplane was noted by Lincoln LaPaz, astronomer at Fairmount College. The professor stated that the meteor was a bright blue color until it exploded, when it burst into leaping flames of red, like an airplane afire, as it dashed downward from the heavens.

Winfield (Ks.) Daily Courier, 6-9-1920, p. 4.

The reports state that the meteor fell in a field a mile west of Okmulgee. It was watched by hundreds of persons there as it fell land all roads leading to the spot where the meteor fell, and which was still blazing an hour and a half later, were clogged with automobiles filled with people who hurried out to watch the meteor burn.

One observer said the meteor fell from high in the sky coming through the clouds with great speed and leaving a tail of light several hundred feet high. There was a loud hissing sound as it fell, he stated. It gave off a white light until close to the ground when it exploded and turned to a reddish color, according to his report.

From observations made by acquaintances, Lincoln La Paz, astronomer and instructor in physics at Fairmount College, gathered that the downward path of the meteor was almost vertical, and was fifty miles in the air when it exploded. He thought it fell 111 miles southeast, which would be near Okmulgee.

Explosions of meteors, he explained were caused by coming into sudden contact with cold air, the atmosphere at the point where he believed the explosion of Tuesday night's meteor being about 400 degrees below zero, Farenheit, or "absolute zero," Mr. La Paz said. Hissing of a large celestial body moving with immeasurable rapidity through space, Mr. La Paz continued, was audible for 400 miles in each direction.

The object descended and seemingly crashed in an empty field west of Okmulgee, Oklahoma, at about 9 p.m. Shortly after the crash landing, all the roads leading to the spot where the object crashed were "clogged with persons in motor cars who went to watch," said newspaper accounts.

Near the supposed crash site, a local merchant named Joe H. Craig and his wife were driving in an automobile west of Okmulgee when the sky lit up and they saw the "ball of fire" streak over them and crash within 200 yards of their car.

The headline in *The Okfuskee (OK.) County News* on June 10 said, "Oklahoma Visited by

Monster Meteor." The article pointed out that residents of Sapulpa, Oklahoma, were convinced that the meteor was actually a "shell" containing a message sent to Earth by the inhabitants of Mars.

The article said, "At Sapulpa, a large searching party headed by Prof C J Foster science instructor in the high school is making a thorough search of the fields east of the city in the belief that a note from Mars may have been sent in a shell arrangement."

Searchers looking for a "hole" marking the meteor's crash site were disappointed, as no such trace was discovered. "That the meteor was of a gaseous nature and may never have hit the earth is the conclusion of some including an astronomer in Muskogee."

Some residents near the crash site reported smelling fumes and feeling earth tremors.

In the days following the crash, as the searches continued without finding physical traces on the ground, a dispute arose as to what town had actually been the landing site of the "meteor." Okmulgee, which claimed to have received the object, may not have been the actual location of the landing. Other towns in both Oklahoma and Arkansas claimed that the strange object landed within their boundaries.

One local newspaper declared, "It is probable that the explosion threw parts of the meteorite in many directions even so far distant as Okmulgee. This would account for the many diverse claims of observers as to the direction in which the visitor was traveling."

Lincoln LaPaz, 1922 Photo from The Wichita (Ks.) Eagle, 4-23-1922, p. 21

So, in the end, no trace was found, and the strange object that was called a "meteor" may have been something else entirely, and it may have landed in a remote location nowhere near Okmulgee. Could it have been a UFO? Its strange flight path and the reported sharp right turn it made during its flight would suggest something other than a meteor.

This event is especially notable because of the involvement of future government UFO investigator Lincoln LaPaz. The *Wichita (Ks.) Beacon* for June 9, 1920, said, "The meteor was seen by Wichita people about nine o'clock last night. Many thought it was a burning airplane. Lincoln Lapaz, Wichita astronomer and head of the physics department of Fairmount College, has gone to Okmulgee to study the charred remains of the meteor, which has been taken in charge by the government."

By the 1950s, LaPaz was one of America's pre-eminent investigators of both meteors and unidentified objects seen descending through the Earth's atmosphere. *Wikipedia* states, "In ufology, LaPaz's name is often associated with UFO investigations on behalf of the military during the late 1940s and early 1950s. These include the Roswell UFO incident of 1947, the N.M. green fireballs that began in late 1948 and continued through the 1950s, and the search for near-Earth orbiting satellites in 1954 along with fellow N.M. astronomer Clyde Tombaugh."

Of special note is LaPaz's reported involvement in the world's most famous UFO story – the alleged crash of a flying saucer near Roswell, New Mexico, in July 1947. "Regarding the 1947 Roswell incident, at least three witnesses, including two involved with Army and Air Force counterintelligence, claimed that LaPaz was brought in after the Roswell UFO incident to interview witnesses and reconstruct the trajectory of the crash object," according to *Wikipedia.*

LaPaz was also involved in investigating another famous and well-documented UFO case. "In 1964 LaPaz was also involved peripherally in the investigation of the famous Socorro UFO incident, in which a Socorro policeman named Lonnie Zamora saw a small egg-shaped object land, saw two humanoid figures near the object, and then when he approached to within 50 feet, the object blasted off and rapidly disappeared. LaPaz interviewed Zamora and vouched for him as a witness."

Back in June 1920, Lincoln LaPaz was a 23-year-old astronomer, serving as the head of the physics department at Fairmount College in Wichita, Kansas. Even at this early date, he had a keen interest in all things entering the Earth's atmosphere from outer space, whether known or unknown. Many UFO researchers strongly suspect that there was "another side" to LaPaz – associated with his top-secret efforts to help the U.S. government investigate reports that the Earth was being visited by extraterrestrials.

LaPaz reportedly made comments to the effect that the 1947 Roswell object was extraterrestrial in origin and that the mysterious "green fireballs" seen throughout the Southwest in 1965 were anomalies that held a key to understanding UFOs. In the context of his later UFO investigations, his involvement in the 1920 Oklahoma UFO sightings is fascinating. LaPaz passed away on October 19, 1985, at the age of 88.

SKIES LIGHTED BY BRILLIANT METEOR

Finally Lands in Field One Mile West of Okmulgee, Oklahoma.

Kansas City, June 9.—A meteor of intense brilliancy swept across the Southwest last night, lighted up the skies over several states and fell a burning mass near Okmulgee, Okla.

The phenomenon, which was seen here, also was witnessed by hundreds of persons in southern Missouri, Kansas, Oklahoma and Arkansas, according to reports received in Kansas City.

At Okmulgee the roads leading to the spot where the meteor fell were clogged with persons in motor cars who went to watch the meteor burn itself out.

C. B. Smith, an astronomy authority at Muskogee, expressed the belief that the meteor was thrown off from a destroyed planet between Jupiter and Mars. It appeared to travel from west to east, Professor Smith said.

Other persons who saw it declared almost a minute elapsed from the time the meteor appeared until it completed the arc of its travel.

Oklahoma City, June 9.—An enormous meteor, which lighted up the sky over eastern Oklahoma and western Arkansas and sent a thrill of apprehension through hundreds who saw it, fell at 9 o'clock last night a short distance west of Okmulgee, Okla., according to a message received here.

From Fort Smith, Ark., came a report that the meteor had caused considerable apprehension among the people of that section, who believed it had struck near Red Oak, Okla., about 25 miles distant, and a number of people in automobiles left from Wilburton, Okla., and near-by towns for Red Oak to lend any aid necessary.

Tulsa, Okla., reported the meteor when it passed over that city appeared to be within a few hundred yards of the earth and that the lower and heavier portion was of a greenish blue color, followed by a long wedge-shaped tail. As it approached the earth, the report states, the head apparently separated into four parts but remained together as a mass and that during the last few seconds of the fall the southern sky was lighted with a blue-green flash.

Hundreds of people here witnessed the meteor in its flight across the sky and reported it appeared to be far to the east.

Shawnee, Okla., reported the meteor appeared the shape of an incandescent light and left a trail of red stars in its wake and that motorists had reported the meteor had apparently fallen about 10 miles northeast of that place.

At Bartlesville, Okla., hundreds of people witnessed the meteor as it fell and said that it lighted up the city with a brilliant bluish color for half a minute.

Okmulgee, Okla., June 9.—A meteor, whose flight to earth was watched by hundreds here for nearly a minute, fell in a field one mile west of this city at 9 o'clock last night. All roads leading to the spot where the meteor fell and which is still blazing are clogged with automobile loads of people who hurried out to watch the meteor burn.

The meteor came from a destroyed planet between Jupiter and Mars, according to Professor C. B. Smith, professor of astronomy here. He said frequently this planet throws off bits that hurtle through space and that friction in passing through the air at tremendous speed ignites them and they usually are burned to ashes before they strike the earth.

The meteor appeared to travel from the west to the east, Professor Smith said.

Tulsa, Shawnee, Bartlesville, Okla., and Fort Smith, Ark., report seeing the meteor.

Joe H. Craig, a local merchant, and his wife were driving in an automobile west of the city when the sky suddenly lighted. They saw the ball of fire overhead, Craig said, and his wife became hysterical.

The meteor struck within 200 yards of their car.

Hundreds of residents of Little Rock saw the meteor shortly before 9 o'clock. While many were aware that it was a meteor, among the superstitious the usual fears of the "world coming to an end" and other calamitous happenings prevailed.

Arkansas (Little Rock) Democrat, 6-9-1920, p. 11.

3
IOWA
UFO CRASH

Iowa City, Iowa
July 4, 1920

ON THE MORNING OF July 7, 1920, residents
of Iowa City, Iowa, opened their local newspaper
and read an amazing story about a mysterious
airship having crashed in the woods north of town.
The headline proclaimed, "Mystery Veils Fallen
Airship. Where Did Pilot and Motor Go When
Plane Fell in Woods Along Iowa River?" While
the article may have been news to some in Iowa
City, word about the mysterious crash, which
happened three days earlier, had already gotten
around town, and the paper noted that "many Iowa
City people have gone to the river to investigate the

strange veil of unusualness that enshrouds the discovery."

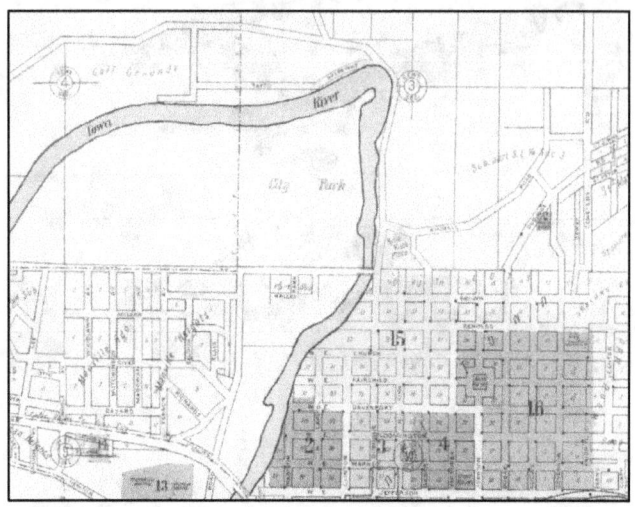

1920 map of Iowa City showing the general area of the crash

The principal eyewitness in this case was a veteran railroad shipping worker, an "expressman," named J. J. Beranek, whose job it was to ensure the safe delivery of gold or currency, being shipped by railroad, typically in safes or strongboxes located in the train's "express car." Beranek was working north of Iowa City near an area known as "Butler's Landing," when he witnessed the strange object streaking down from the sky and falling in the woods near the Iowa River, on the property of Captain S. D. Pryce and Charles Weber.

A woman living in the area stated that she saw the object "shooting earthward," according to a July 7th article in the *Iowa City Press-Citizen*. Others in the area stated they heard a loud sound described as a "reverberation" associated with the fall of the airship.

Butler's Landing, circa 1920 (Public Domain)

When Beranek went to see what had fallen in the woods, he found a "machine" that lay wrecked upon the ground, with no sign of a pilot anywhere in the area. Also, curiously, there was no "engine" – in other words, the craft did not seem to have a mechanism for propulsion.

That the mysterious airship had no pilot was described as "oddly inexplicable," and the townspeople theorized that the pilot might have fallen into the river or the woods as the object streaked down to the ground. The newspaper article states, "If the pilot fell out of the machine, as it fell – and a woman in the neighborhood avers she saw it shooting earthward, he may have dropped in the river, but no sign of him appears in the grove or anywhere else. Such a plunge into the Iowa River, to death by drowning, or being crushed, is possible, perhaps, but it is oddly inexplicable."

Also reported as being "extraordinary" was the fact that no engine was found in the wreckage of the fallen airship. Said the newspaper, "The loss of the engine, however, seems without explanation. If the machine blew up, and some people state a reverberation was heard, indicating an explosion, the airship, surely, ought to have been torn to pieces, more than the engine, destroyed to a point of utter obliteration."

MYSTERY VEILS FALLEN AIRSHIP

Where Did Pilot and Motor Go, When Plane Fell in Woods Along Iowa River?

J. J. Beranek, the veteran express-man, describes the startling discovery in the woods, near Butler's Landing in the woods owned by Capt. S. D. Pryce and Charles Weber, along the Iowa river, north of town.

The machine lay in the woods, after a seeming Fourth of July flight and the wrecked, if not burned ship, was extraordinary without a motor.

Pilot is Missing.

If the pilot fell out of the machine, as it fell—and a woman in the neighborhood avers she saw it shooting earthward, he may have dropped in the river, but no sign of him appears in the grove or anywhere else.

Could Pilot Be Drowned?

Such a plunge into the Iowa river, to death by drowning, or being crushed, is possible, perhaps, but it is oddly inexplicable. The loss of the engine, however, seems without explanation. If the machine blew up, and some people state a reverberation was heard, indicating an explosion, the airship, surely, ought to have been torn to pieces, more than the engine, destroyed to a point of utter obliteration.

Mystery Puzzles Many.

Mystery envelops the find, and many Iowa City people have gone up the river to investigate the strange veil of unusualness that enshrouds the discovery.

Iowa City Press-Citizen, July 7, 1920, p. 2

Nothing further is reported in the newspaper article, and the only follow-up article was published a day later, stating that the mystery remained unsolved. What happened to the strange wreckage is unknown.

The historical record shows that the persons mentioned in this story were actual people. Beranek, in addition to working as an expressman, also worked as a "drayman," delivering beer for a local brewery. He was married and had relatives in Davenport, Iowa, located 60 miles east of Iowa City. Captain S. D. Pryce was a retired fireman and "respected" citizen of Iowa City.

We find that this chapter relates to the previous two in interesting ways. First of all, it was the second possible UFO crash in less than a month's time, with another having preceded this one near Okmulgee, Oklahoma, on June 8th. In that case, witnesses mistook the potential alien craft for a "monster meteor" that was magically able to change its course! It's also interesting that the UFO incident related in the first chapter happened a month earlier in the nearby town of Mount Pleasant, Iowa, located about 50 miles south of Iowa City.

On October 28, 1973, *The Hawk Eye*, a newspaper in Burlington, Iowa, ran a story from 75-year-old Clark Linch, who claimed to have encountered a UFO in Mount Pleasant, Iowa, in 1920, when he was 22 years old.

Linch told the newspaper that he was convinced he saw an extraterrestrial spacecraft while he was fishing at about 10 a.m. on June 3, 1920. He remembered the date because it happened to be his birthday, and he had taken some time from working on his father's farm to go fishing.

While fishing, Linch saw an egg-shaped object the size of a "cream can" land silently about fifteen feet from where he was seated on the riverbank. The translucent, blue object "sat there" for about fifteen minutes, "not bothering him – nor he bothering it," according to the newspaper article.

The small size of the object, and its apparent light weight, seemed to preclude that any intelligent beings were inside of it. "It couldn't have been occupied by intelligent life as we know it," he said. "I didn't know what to believe about it at the time, and I still don't. I've concluded that it wasn't anything from Earth."

Is it possible that the ship that crashed in the vicinity of Iowa City was similar to the unmanned drone sighted in Mount Pleasant, only much larger? As it stands, since neither craft appeared to have living creatures in them, it seems that both might have been probes or drones sent to our planet for surveillance or reconnaissance.

4

UFO LANDS IN COTTON FIELD

Bethel, North Carolina
September 1920

A FASCINATING CLOSE ENCOUNTER of the third kind from 1920 is mentioned in "UFO Roundup," Volume 7, Number 28 (July 9, 2002), edited by Joseph Trainer of *UFOinfo.com.*

The incident took place in September of 1920, while the harvest was in full swing on the cotton farms around Bethel, North Carolina, a small town on Highway 13 about 60 miles east of Raleigh. The eyewitness in the case kept the story to herself until 1991, when she told the story to her grandson, Gil Rodriguez.

The principal eyewitness is identified as 14-year-old "Nicora B." She, along with her family, were day laborers in North Carolina, and as such, the family worked from sunrise to sunset for the three months beginning in September, which is the busiest time of year for cotton harvesting.

North Carolina Cotton Harvest (Public Domain)

Nicora and her family walked methodically down the long rows of cotton plants, plucking the white bolls from the plants, and stuffing them in their tote sacks. Although the day of the UFO incident started off uneventfully, full of the usual tedium and back-breaking labor, it ended up as something altogether different. The events of that day would live on in Nicora's memory for the rest of her life.

The encounter began early one afternoon while Nicora and her relatives were picking "high cotton," which is found atop the taller cotton plants. Suddenly, the family noticed a large, metallic-silver object flying across the sky over the cotton farm.

"It looked like two pie pans placed together, lip to lip," Nicora said in 1991 when she disclosed the incident to her grandson. She also stated that the craft was larger than a typical automobile.

Artist's Rendition of UFO

Nicora said the silvery UFO "zigzagged across the sky" and finally "came to rest in the field in front of them."

The startled farmworkers watched the amazing sight, noticing that a door or portal on the ship was starting to open. Soon, two humanoid creatures appeared out of the ship's interior and moved down to the ground. Nicora described the beings as "little bald white men." They were about the size and stature of an 8 to 10-year-old child. Nicora said, "They were the size of little boys, but their faces seemed older."

As the creatures stood looking at Nicora and her family, they pointed "short sticks" at them. What this gesture was meant to accomplish is unknown, but the sticks were obviously not weapons. Might the sticks have been some type of camera or probe?

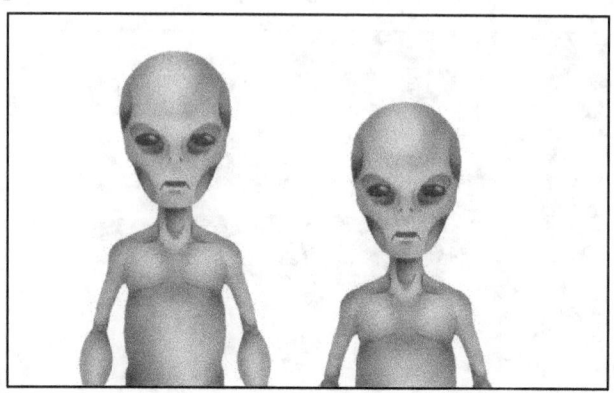

Artist's Depiction of UFO Occupants

One of the strange beings then brought out a different type of tool that looked "something like a shovel" and began using it to dig and poke into the soil near his feet. Using the tool, he scooped out a sample of dirt and put it inside a bag he was carrying. Finally, the creature picked up a small plant and also placed it in his bag.

After the specimen collection was completed, the two humanoids once again pointed the odd "sticks" at Nicora and her family and "walked backwards" into their ship, keeping the farmworkers fully in their view at all times.

Within moments, the UFO powered up and took off into sky, resuming the zigzagging motion they had observed earlier, before it finally disappeared in the same direction from which it had come.

In telling the story to her grandson, Nicora said that the family believed what happened might have been some kind of U.S. government experiment. "We all thought it had something to do with the government," she said.

The family members continued talking about the incident for "a little while" after it happened but then went back to work. In order to make their day's wages, they could not afford to take any more time away from their tasks.

A search of U.S. Census data for 1920 did not find any entries for a "Nicora B." However, it is important to note that many people, including migrant workers, minorities, and immigrants, were not counted in the Census. It is also unknown if the initial B refers to Nicroa's married name or her maiden name.

If Nicora B. was 14 at the time of the incident, she would have been born in 1906 or 1907. Our search of the census found two Nicoras that were born in 1906 – Nicora A. Gonzales of New Mexico and Nicora Lombardo of Brooklyn, N.Y. Born in 1907 was Nicora Pisani of Bronx, N.Y. It is difficult, given the lack of further evidence, to verify the identity of "Nicora B."

In any case, this account provided not only a fascinating sighting of a traditional flying saucer type UFO, but what sounded to be alien Greys as well.

UFOs IN THE ROARING TWENTIES

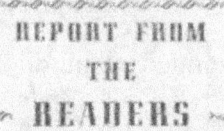

REPORT FROM THE READERS

UFO MOTHER SHIP

I work nights and usually take a walk around noon. On May 27, 1955, I was striding along, watching the path in front of me, when suddenly the sun seemed to go behind a cloud. That immediately struck me as strange for it was a bright, hot day, without a cloud in the sky.

I looked up and saw a huge object suspended about 2,000 feet in the air. It seemed to be the size of an ocean liner. It was not a blimp because I am familiar with them and this object was entirely too large. It made no sound, released no smoke, just hung suspended. It was oval in shape, colored black, silver and red, and seemed to have windows.

I looked at it for at least three minutes, too scared to move. Then I heard a car coming and flagged the motorist. When I looked at the sky again the object was gone. It disappeared in the few seconds I took my eyes off it.

I told the motorist what I had seen and he said he, his wife, and his mother had seen exactly the same type of object at Palermo, Calif., two years before. He thought the object may have been connected with the Brush Creek flying saucer incident. We discussed my experience for an hour and a half at the side of the road and concluded that what I had seen was a mother ship.

At 9 A.M. on June 1, 1955, I saw the object again. This time my mother and father also saw it. We were at our home in Oroville. The object appeared to be at the same height as before and was moving toward the east. It was visible for about five minutes.

My mother, remarking that seeing is believing, said that in all her 55 years on earth she had never seen anything like that moving object. Dad said the same. — *Bob Wright, Oroville, Calif.*

PEARL IN THE SKY

Back in 1930 I saw an oval object in the sky over Bainbridge Island, Wash. It was a fair and windy day, with scattered clouds going from north to south. I saw the object distinctly against the blue sky when clouds were not in the way. It was three times smaller than the moon and looked like a magnificent pearl in the sky.

I am positive the object was not a reflection nor any sort of electrical phenomenon like ball lightning. It hovered high above the clouds and showed no signs of making headway. Dark clouds presently covered this amazing object from my view. — *Larry Reynolds, San Pedro, Calif.*

Report from the Readers — December 1955

FISHING FOR UFOS
Near Freeport, Texas
October 1920

A SIGHTING OF FOUR flying discs occurred in October 1920 along the Texas Gulf Coast, about 50 miles north of Freeport, Texas. The witness was a fisherman named C. B. Alves, who was out doing some early-morning fishing with friends when the group spotted the unusual sight. It happened at 3 o'clock in the morning (which, probably not coincidentally, is when one is most likely to encounter an alien being based on cumulative data over the years).

Alves stated that each of the four craft looked "like two big silver plates set edge to edge." They seemed to be about 25 feet in diameter and about 10 feet thick at the center. The objects were not spinning.

Alves watched as one of the discs approached to within 100 yards of where he stood before it veered off, climbed, and sped away to the south. Three additional discs followed the first one.

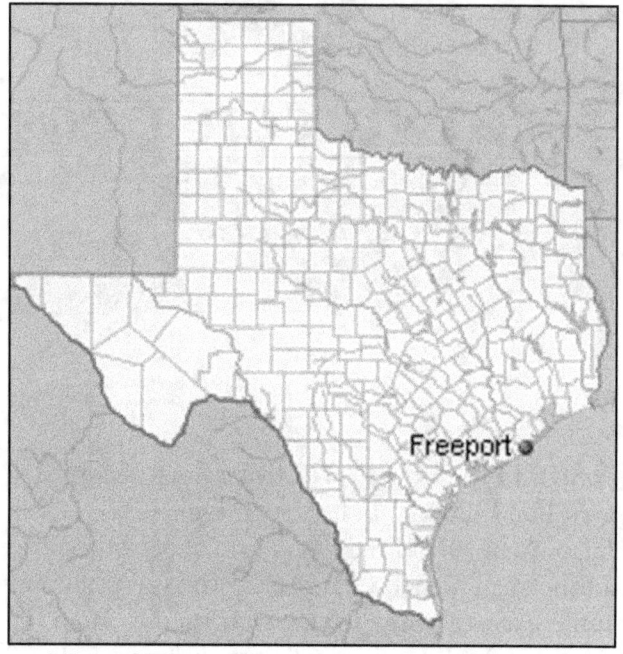

Map of Texas Showing Location of Freeport

All four discs appeared identical, except for the color of the light emanating from each object. Alves said the first and last discs showed a brilliant pink pastel light, and the second and third displayed a pale green but were equally brilliant.

After being seen by Alves and his group, the fleet of UFOs zoomed away and disappeared.

The account of Alves' sighting was published in the February 1955 edition of America's leading

paranormal publication, *Fate Magazine*, in its "Report from the Readers" section. A report on the case appeared in Jerome Clark's *The UFO Encyclopedia: The Phenomenon from the Beginning*, 3rd edition (2018).

Interestingly, as UFO sightings increased exponentially in the 1950s, *Fate Magazine* began to receive numerous UFO reports from its readers, relating experiences that happened in earlier decades, including the 1920s. Clearly, people who had UFO encounters prior to 1947 did not understand what they were seeing and struggled to put this encounter into words. They referred to "mystery aircraft," "unexplained lights," "shining orbs," and other such terminology.

UFO witnesses of the earlier decades did not have the vocabulary that came along after UFO sightings exploded in 1947. But, after 1947, they went back in their memories and relived their prior experiences, better understanding what happened to them in the new context of what had begun occurring throughout the world after 1947.

Consequently, a number of the UFO stories featured in this book were not reported by the witnesses when they occurred (in the 1920s). Instead, they were typically reported in the decades following 1947.

UFOs IN THE ROARING TWENTIES

Incident 119: A.D. 1920. At a location on the Gulf Coast, about 50 miles from Freeport, Texas, an observer saw a rapidly-moving disc while fishing at approximately 2.00 a.m. one Autumn morning. The object seemed headed directly for him, but when some 100 yards distant, it turned south and could then see three additional discs following it. All seemed to be of identical size and shape, although the light they emitted varied from brilliant pink to pale green. The witness described each object as "two big silver plates set edge to edge". Each appeared to be about 25 feet in diameter and 10 feet thick at the centre. No spinning motions were observed. The objects began climbing as they headed south, and faded out in the distance.

(Fate, February 1955, "report from the readers").

Summary from The UFO Register, v. 9, 1978.

A search of the historical record for the name C.B. Alves yielded inconclusive results. The surname "Alves" was well represented in Texas in the 1920 U.S. Census, as was its variant "Alvis." But having only initials for the first name and middle name make identification a bit more difficult. We found a "Canrodo Alves" who lived in Terrell, Texas, about 300 miles northwest of Freeport. Canrodo, born in 1909, would have been 11 years old in 1920. There were quite a number of other males with the surname "Alves" in Texas, but none with the initials "C.B." Then again, the witness may not have been a Texas resident and may have been visiting from a neighboring state, such as Louisiana or Oklahoma.

ROCKET-SHAPED UFO

Billings, Montana
1920

IN MAY 1954, *Fate Magazine* published a "Special Saucer Issue," featuring the article "Hunt for the Saucers." Among the many interesting UFO encounters reported in this special issue was a fascinating story of a UFO sighting in 1920 near Billings, Montana.

The article was submitted by World War II veteran Stanley Clason, who was ten years old at the time that the sighting occurred in 1920.

Although he did not remember the exact date of the incident, Clason's story was nonetheless remarkable. A resident of Billings, Montana, at the time, Clason was visiting his uncle's ranch north of Billings.

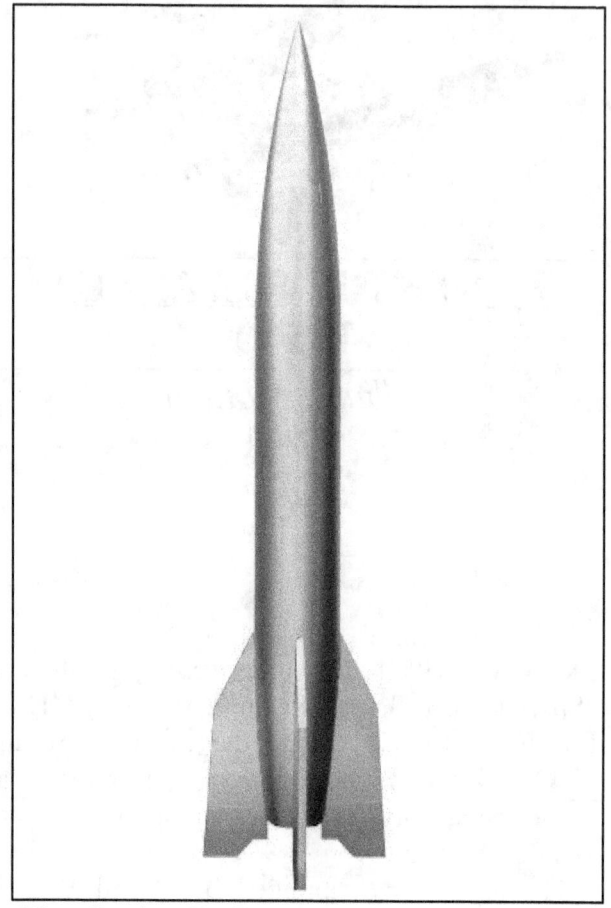

Silver Rocket Similar to Nazi Design of the 1940s

Walking across a pasture, he noticed something moving in the sky above him. Focusing his view, he saw a strange, silver-colored cylindrical object moving from the northwest and heading toward the southeast at an extremely high speed, perhaps three times faster than a modern jet airplane.

Clason described the object as a "long, slim, pointed shape" that was "silvery in color." The description sounds almost like a rocket or a missile, a technology that did not exist at the time.

> Incident 118: A.D. 1920 (?). A 10-year old boy in northern Montana (exact site not named) observed a silvery cylindrical object moving rapidly from northwest to southeast, at an apparently high altitude in a cloudless sky. The speed was estimated to be two or three times that of a modern jet airplane.
>
> (Fate, April 1954, "report from the readers").

Summary from The UFO Register, v. 9, 1978.

Rockets of this type were first invented in 1926 by American physicist Robert H. Goddard, who launched 34 rockets between 1926 and 1941. Goddard's rocket designs were later stolen by Nazi Germany and were used to create a number of military rockets during World War II.

So, to be clear, rockets of the kind that carried warheads or payloads of any type, did not exist in 1920. Also, there were no known inventors working on rockets in Montana, or actually anywhere in the U.S. in 1920.

Stanley Clason, 53, Dies in California

HARDIN—Stanley Clason, 53, former Billings resident, died in Palo Alto, Calif., Saturday of a lung and heart condition. He was returning to Montana after being treated in New Mexico for several years.

Mr. Clason was born Sept. 12, 1910, in Custer, S.D., a son of Mr. and Mrs. John Clason. He grew up in Montana and was graduated from Chinook High School. He was a veteran of the Second World War. He was a member of the First Methodist Church.

He is survived by his mother, Mrs. Nettie Crawford of Basin, Wyo.; three sons, Dale of 8 Riley Drive, Billings, Donald of Basin and Louis Dean of Los Angeles, Calif.; a brother, and four sisters.

Funeral services are tentatively set for 2 p.m. Monday, with the Rev. Don Hamilton of the First Methodist Church officiating. Burial will be in Custer Battlefield National Cemetery.

Bullis Funeral Home is in charge of arrangements.

The Billings (Montana) Gazette, 4-30-1964, p. 6.

The witness description did not make mention of any exhaust coming from the rocket's tail section. Neither did it reference any tailfins or markings of any kind on the rocket. So what the object could have been remains a puzzle to this day. The eyewitness, Stanley Clason, passed away on April 25, 1964, at the age of 53. His sighting was included in Jerome Clark's *The UFO Encyclopedia: The Phenomenon from the Beginning*, 3rd edition (2018).

7

UFO ABDUCTIONS AT SEA

Atlantic Ocean
January 1921

ON JANUARY 31, 1921, the U.S. ocean-going vessel *Carroll A. Deering*, a five-masted commercial schooner out of Boston, was found run aground off Cape Hatteras, North Carolina in 1921 with the crew nowhere to be found. The Deering's vanishing, which remains unsolved to this day, was only one of several mysterious disappearances of ships and ship crews that were reported in 1921.

The February 1, 1921, edition of the *Boston Globe* stated, "Mystery surrounds the wreck of the Boston five-masted schooner Carroll A. Deering, which was driven on the beach at Hatteras Shoals with no one on board. In command of Capt. Wormell of Bath, and carrying a crew of 12 men, the vessel left Rio Janeiro Dec. 2 and Barbados Jan. 9, bound for Norfolk, in ballast. She was sighted off Hatteras abandoned and with all her sails set before she was swept ashore."

The Caroll A. Deering, as seen from the Cape Lookout lightship on January 28, 1921 (U.S. Coast Guard photo)

The riveting account continued, "The Coast Guard crew who went out to the vessel could find no trace of the crew, and it is believed that they were taken off by some passing steamer." The problem is, as investigations over the past century have shown, none of the crew were ever found or accounted for in any manner.

Although no crew members were found aboard the ship, searchers did find a parrot below decks that did a lot of "screeching" but spoke no words that might help determine what happened. The *Boston Globe* of February 3, 1921, also noted the following curious fact, "A swarm of seagulls has been around the ship since Monday morning,

MYSTERY IN WRECK OF BOSTON SCHOONER

Swept Ashore With All Sails Set—No One Aboard

Mystery surrounds the wreck of the Boston five-masted schooner Carroll A. Deering, which was driven on the beach at Hatteras Shoals with no one on board. In command of Capt Wormell, of Bath, and carrying a crew of 12 men, the vessel left Rio Janeiro Dec 2 and Barbados Jan 9, bound for Norfolk, in ballast. She was sighted off Hatteras abandoned and with all her sails set before she was swept ashore.

The Coast Guard crew who went out to the vessel could find no trace of the crew, and it is believed that they were taken off by some passing steamer.

The Carroll A. Deering was built at Bath in 1919, and was valued at about $150,000. The owners are Carroll & Thurlow of this city. The schooner is 255 feet long, 44.3 feet beam, 25.3 feet depth of hold, with a net tonnage of 1878 tons and a gross tonnage of 2114. She is only partially insured.

The Boston Globe, Feb. 1, 1921, Page 2.

which has increased the superstitious mutterings of old salts, already sufficiently impressed by the finding of a vessel unharmed, with all sails set and no one on board."

S. S. Hewitt, Union Sulphur Co., Sabine, Texas

Also intriguing about this case is the fact that the crew of the *Deering* appeared to be preparing to have a meal together when something sudden and unexpected happened. "Food in the galley was set out like it was being prepared for the next day's meal," according to the article "The Unsolved Mystery of the Carroll A. Deering, the Outer Banks' Most Famous Ghost Ship" by Meghan Overdeep in *Southern Living* magazine.

Whatever happened to the Deering occurred out at sea during a strong storm. The initial theory was that the crew had tried to escape the gale on lifeboats, since no lifeboats were found on the ship. However, no traces of the lifeboats or crew were ever found.

What seems clear is that the *Carroll A. Deering* encountered something unexpected and possibly unexplained. In the midst of the encounter, the crew tried to abandon ship, but their attempt was clearly unsuccessful. If the ship did encounter a UFO, the crew's efforts to leave the vicinity of their ship did not help them avoid being "taken."

Paranormal researcher Charles Fort, in his 1931 book *Lo!*, was the first to raise the possibility that the disappearance of the *Deering* was an anomaly that might not have an Earthly explanation. Fort wrote, "Nobody aboard. Everything was in good condition. The circumstance that attracted most attention was that the crew had disappeared about the time a meal was to be served."

In his book, Fort theorized that perhaps the crew of the *Deering* might have been "teleported" from the vicinity of their ship to an unknown location.

"If there is a selective force, which transports stones exclusively, or larvae, and nothing but larvae, or transports living things of various sizes, but nothing but living things, such a selective force might affect a number of human beings, leaving no trace, because unaffective to everything else."

But later, Fort concedes that the answer may not be that the crew was teleported, "But I suggest that, with our hints of Teleportation, we are on the wrong track. Crews of vessels have disappeared, and vessels have disappeared. It may be that something of which the inhabitants of this Earth know nothing, is concerned in these disappearances or seizures.... It may be that constructions from somewhere else [i.e. UFOs] have appeared upon this Earth and have seized crews of this earth's ships."

"The case is a favorite of paranormal and Bermuda Triangle hobbyists and has gained a reputation as one of the truly great maritime mysteries," says *Wikipedia.*

On June 21st and 22nd, 1921, the *New York Times* reported on several other strange mysteries involving ships at sea. Some people believed that Russia, whose Soviet regime was just coming to power, was responsible for incidents of piracy, where U.S. ships and their crews were captured and forced to sail to Russia, never to be seen again. However, this theory was never proven, and no evidence was ever found that the Soviets had been responsible for the spate of missing ships in 1921.

At almost the exact same time that the Deering went missing, another mysterious disappearance was reported involving the steamer *S.S. Hewitt* of Portland, Maine, owned by the Union Sulphur Company of New York. While traveling from Sabine Pass in Port Arthur, Texas, to Boston and then Portland, the *Hewitt*, laden with a cargo of sulfur, suddenly and mysteriously vanished off the face of the Earth, along with her entire crew of 42 sailors. It was last contacted by radio on January 25, 1921.

The *Chattanooga News* of Tennessee reported on February 9, 1921: "In the early morning of February [2], coast guardsmen at Atlantic City reported they saw a glaring flash in the Atlantic Ocean followed a moment later by a tremendous explosion. The nature of the cargo of the Hewitt has led to fears that the flash and explosion reported by the guardsmen may have been caused by an accident in the missing steamer. But no wreckage of any vessel has drifted ashore to an Atlantic port or has been reported by coast guardsmen."

The *Sunday Morning Star* of Wilmington, North Carolina, reported on February 6, 1921: "Wednesday night (Feb. 2) coast guards at Atlantic City reported hearing an explosion and seeing a flash about twenty miles off shore. They said at the time they believed some vessel had been blown up. The *Hewitt*'s course would take her past Atlantic City."

The report of a "glaring flash" is incredibly intriguing if one views the disappearance of the ship as possibly resulting from a UFO encounter. Could the entire ship and its crew have been somehow transported from the ocean onto a hovering spacecraft? Was the "explosion" something that happened as the ship was moved from one dimension or time to another?

Authorities conducted an exhaustive search for the ship, retracing its entire voyage from Port Arthur, Texas, to a point about 250 nautical miles north of Jupiter Inlet, Florida. The extensive and careful search yielded no results of any kind – no wreckage, no bodies, no clues. Although some observers blamed piracy for the ship's disappearance, the *New York Times* observed, "Officials concede that it is difficult to believe that acts of piracy could be committed in and near the territorial waters of the United States in this day."

The June 22, 1921 edition of the *New York Times* ran the headline "Almost Simultaneous Disappearance Without a Trace Regarded as Significant." The article pointed out that prior to the *Deering* and the *Hewitt* vanishing, two other ships also disappeared – the Spanish steamer *Yute* and the Russian ship *Albyan*.

"The *Yute* sailed from Baltimore for Dunkirk on Oct. 1 [1920] .... Government vessels and other ships put out to her assistance but were never able to get any trace of her," reported the *Times*.

"The *Albyan* sailed from Norfolk for Gothenberg [Sweden] on Oct 1. She has never been heard from, and not the slightest trace of any wreckage from her has been found."

The article also mentions several other ships that were reported missing, including the Italian steamer *Monte San Michele*, the Brazilian steamer *Esperanza de Larrinaga*, and the British tank steamer *Ottawa*.

Two days later, the *New York Times* reported that the government had added several more ships to the list of the missing, bringing the total to over a dozen. "Weather Bureau officials came forward tonight with the theory that some of the dozen or more ships reported to have disappeared mysteriously in the North Atlantic may have been lost in the series of unusually severe storms which are known to have swept that area in the first weeks of February 1921."

So, in the midst of atmospheric disturbances, flashes, and explosions, a number of ocean-going vessels and their crews entirely disappeared from existence early in 1921. Despite extensive investigations, nothing of their whereabouts was ever discovered. It was as if they had been lifted off the face of the earth and transported ... somewhere else.

In Steven Spielberg's 1977 science fiction film *Close Encounters of the Third Kind*, extraterrestrials bring back to Earth a number of human beings that they have abducted from our planet over the many centuries of human existence. Included in this group are pilots, sailors, soldiers, and regular civilians. One might argue that the filmmaker could have easily included the crews of 1921's missing ships in this large crowd of abductees returned to their home planet. Is it possible that the crews of these disappeared ships are still out there ... somewhere?

8

THE CASE OF THE
TWO SUNS

Mount Hamilton, California
August 7, 1921

IMAGINE BEING ON a planet in a solar system with two suns. Looking up at the sky, we would see two bright objects shining light down upon our Earth. On one day in 1921, many people looked up at the sky and thought they saw a second sun – a very bright object located alongside the sun with which we are all familiar. What is most amazing about this sighting is that it was witnessed by astronomers, who are highly trained observers of the sky. As we look at history, when astronomers say that they observed something strange, it is almost always a report worth looking into.

UFOs IN THE ROARING TWENTIES

At sunset on August 7, 1921, something out of the ordinary was witnessed by a number of observers, including Professor William Wallace Campbell, director of the Lick Observatory, located upon the summit of Mount Hamilton, California.

Lick Observatory on Mt. Hamilton, Circa 1900
(Public Domain)

Although the story of what they saw did not make major headlines and was quickly forgotten, the famous paranormal researcher Charles Fort included the discovery of this "unknown luminous object" in his 1923 book *New Lands* and in his 1931 book *Lo!,* indicating that to him, it was a significant sighting.

Fort called it "a brilliant and conspicuous appearance." He noted that it was not just one of the many "small points on photographic plates" that had been discovered previously and afterward.

The mysterious sighting was discussed in the August 7, 1921 edition of the *Journal of the Royal Astronomical Society of Canada*, in an article by Canadian astronomer Joseph A. Pearce, titled "The Unidentified Bright Object Seen Near the Sun."

Astronomer William Wallace Campbell

In the article, the moment of discovery is described. A party was being held at Campbell's residence located on Mount Hamilton, near the Lick Observatory, when those in attendance at the party noticed something strange in the sky.

One of Campbell's guests, identified only as "Major Chambers", said, "What star is that to the left of the sun?" Another guest, famous American World War I fighter ace Edward Rickenbacker, stated that he had been looking at the "star" for several minutes but had not mentioned it because he supposed it was well known. All of the observers agreed that the unknown object was "star-like."

Astronomer Campbell grabbed a pair of binoculars and continued to observe the object briefly before it "disappeared behind the cloud stratum at the horizon." Also puzzled by the sighting was another of Campbell's guests, noted Princeton astronomer Henry Norris Russell.

Astronomer Henry Norris Russell

All the men were mystified by what they had seen. The two astronomers, Campbell and Russell, concluded that the object was brighter than Venus would have been under similar circumstances. After comparing notes, the two scientists sent the following telegram to the Harvard College Observatory, "Star-like object, certainly brighter than Venus, three degrees east, one degree south, of sun seen several minutes before and at sunset by naked eye. Five observers. Set behind low clouds. Unquestionably celestial object. Chances favor nucleus bright comet, less probably nova."

It was later revealed that other astronomers had also seen the object, including Mr. S. Fellows at Wolverhampton, England, who described it as "reddish" and "elongated towards the sun."

The respected scientific journal *Nature*, in its October 6, 1921 edition, carried this account from yet another observer, "Dr. H. C. Emmert ... states that he saw a bright object in the western sky on August 6 .... The object was fully as bright as Venus in twilight at her greatest brilliancy, and the light was perfectly steady."

In the article from the *Journal of the Royal Astronomical Society of Canada*, the following conclusion was reached, "What was it then, a nova or a comet? Being 40 degrees from the Galactic plane would almost certainly rule out the former. A comet is more feasible. ... Although this hypothesis seems the most likely, the object still remains somewhat of a mystery."

But perhaps the scientific explanation that the world of astronomy was desperately trying to find was not the correct one. This strange object, confirmed by astronomers and seen by many people, remains unexplained to this day.

Photo of Mars
E.S.A & MPS for OSIRIS Team
MPS/UPD/LAM/IAA/RSSD/INTA/UPM/DASP/IDA, CC BY-SA IGO
3.0 / CC BY-SA 3.0-IGO *(https://creativecommons.org/licenses/by-sa/3.0-igo)*

CONTACTING MARS

New York, New York
September 2, 1921

ON THE MORNING of September 2, 1921, residents of New York City awoke to a headline in the *New York Tribune* newspaper stating that one of the world's top scientists, Guglielmo Marconi (1874-1937), had very likely received intelligent signals from the planet Mars. The headline, "Marconi Believes He Received Wireless Message from Mars," had a profound impact because Marconi was well known as the inventor of radio and for his work on wireless telegraphy.

Speaking at the Rotary Club of New York, the London manager of the Marconi Wireless Telegraph Company, J. C. H. MacBeth, stated that

Marconi believed "he had intercepted messages from Mars during recent atmospheric experiments with wireless on board his yacht *Electra* in the Mediterranean."

Guglielmo Marconi, Electrical Engineer & Inventor

According to the *Tribune* article, "Marconi had been unable to conceive any other explanation of the fact that during his experiments he picked up magnetic wave lengths of 150,000 meters, whereas the maximum length of wave produced, in the world today is 14,000 meters."

MacBeth told the newspaper that the signals from Mars could not have been caused by electrical disturbances because they had "regularity." He also said the signals were not intelligible and were possibly in some type of "code."

MacBeth told the newspaper, "The fact is we don't know how far wireless rays will travel. It is not at all impossible or for that matter improbable that some planet, on which the same method we are using has been perfected, may be trying to get into communication with us. We continually hear these high-power taps, delivered with such regularity that it completely dispels any suggestion of their being caused by ordinary electrical activities of the atmosphere. These we have learned to understand and gauge. The signals I am referring to are quite another sort."

He pointed out that hearing the signals did not equate to understanding them. "There is, of course, the language barrier that interposes in our effort to interpret messages from other planets. Still, the Germans were able in three weeks to decipher English code messages used in war time and we were equally successful in deciphering their code."

Could the signals received by Marconi have been coming from wireless stations on Earth? MacBeth said absolutely not. "It has been suggested that these signals might have come from some German or Russian wireless station, but I repeat that there is no station on the face of the globe that is capable of producing them. Also, by international agreement every station and the length of the waves it is capable of producing are known."

According to the *Tribune*, Marconi had previously announced in January 1920 that mysterious signals had been received which appeared to come from another planet and that he was conducting further experiments in an effort to decipher them.

Marconi Believes He Received Wireless Message From Mars

London Manager Tells Club Here of Mysterious Signals Heard on Yacht in Mediterranean; Waves 150,000 Meters in Length Picked Up

J. C. H MacBeth, London manager of the Marconi Wireless Telegraph Compand, Ltd., told several hundred men at a luncheon of the Rotary Club of New York yesterday that Signor Marconi believed he had intercepted messages from Mars during recent atmospheric experiments with wireless on board his yacht Electra in the Mediterranean.

tures and illustrations of various sorts by wireless. The thing has already been done successfully, and it remains only to perfect details for universal use of the method."

Mr. Macbeth also referred to the advantages of the direction finder developed by wireless, which permitted accurate direction of ships at sea and airplanes in foggy weather.

New York Tribune, Sept. 2, 1921, p. 3

The newspaper account concludes by saying, "Prizes aggregating more than a quarter of a million dollars will be won by the scientist who first succeeds in establishing intelligible communication with another planet. The latest of these, $20,000, is offered by the Paris Academy of Science."

Our old friend, paranormal investigator Charlse Fort, also had something to say on Marconi's observations. We'll let Fort have the final word on the case, as penned in his book *New Lands*: "In the summer of 1921, the planet Mars was far from opposition. The magnetic vibrations may have come from some other world."

10

ASTRONOMER SEES LIFE ON THE MOON

Boston, Massachusetts
October 8, 1921

PEOPLE AWOKE ONE October morning in 1921 and read blaring headlines proclaiming that life had been discovered on the surface of the moon! "LIFE EXISTANT ON MOON," screamed the headline on the front page of the *Harrisburg (PA.) Courier.* "HARVARD ASTRONOMER Professor William Henry Pickering Completes Series of Telescopic Observations Which He Asserts Will Prove Moon is Inhabited by Living Creatures -- Declares it Resembles Mars in Some Respects But is Unlike Anything on Our Own Planet."

Harvard Astronomer William Henry Pickering
(Library of Congress)

Professor Pickering was no amateur astronomer letting his imagination run wild. A graduate of the Massachusetts Institute of Technology (MIT), Pickering helped establish Percival Lowell's Flagstaff Observatory in Arizona and did notable work in observations of the sun and the moon. Considered one of the world's leading astronomers of his time, when Pickering released statements concerning the heavens, people listened with great attention.

On October 8, 1921, Pickering announced that after making a series of careful observations of the moon, which included taking telescopic photographs, he had concluded that life existed on the surface of the moon.

The article in the *Harrisburg Courier* clarifies that by "life" Professor Pickering meant plants and possibly insects – not intelligent beings. The article said, "He bases his assertions as to moon life on a series of telescopic photographs of a crater on the moon's surface known as Eratosthenes II, with a circumference of thirty-seven miles. The photographs cover a period from August 1920 to February 1921."

The Crater Eratosthenes (NASA Photo)

Pickering interpreted the various shadows and atmospheric distortions as evidence of plant life at the crater. "Scientific examination of the photographic plates proves. Professor Pickering asserts vast fields of foliage spring up with almost unbelievable rapidity when day begins to dawn on the lunar planet, that these wide sweeps of flora come to a full blossom and then as rapidly wane and disappear, vanishing in a maximum period of eleven and in some places a less number of days. Studies of the photographs disclose great blizzards and snow storms sweep across portions of the moon, that volcanic eruptions are frequent there, that fields of moisture, of mist and fog appear and disappear and that clouds abound."

The article quotes Pickering as saying, "We find there a living world, lying at our very doors, where life in some respects resembles that on Mars, but it is entirely unlike anything on our planet."

Interestingly, the description of the fast-growing lunar vegetation closely resembles that given in the novel *The First Men in the Moon*, written in 1900 by British science fiction writer H. G. Wells, as shown in the following excerpt:

Every moment more of these seed coats ruptured, and even as they did so the swelling pioneers overflowed their rent-distended seed-cases, and passed into the second stage of growth. With a steady assurance, a swift deliberation, these amazing seeds thrust a rootlet downward to the earth and a queer little bundle-like bud into the air. In a little while the whole slope was dotted with minute plantlets standing at attention in the blaze of the sun.

They did not stand for long. The bundle-like buds swelled and strained and opened with a jerk, thrusting out a coronet of little sharp tips, spreading a whorl of tiny, spiky, brownish leaves, that lengthened rapidly, lengthened visibly even as we watched. The movement was slower than any animal's, swifter than any plant's I have ever seen before. How can I suggest it to you—the way that growth went on? The leaf tips grew so that they moved onward even while we looked at them. The brown seed-case shrivelled and was absorbed with an equal rapidity. Have you ever on a cold day taken a thermometer into your warm hand and watched the little thread of mercury creep up the tube? These moon plants grew like that.

In a few minutes, as it seemed, the buds of the more forward of these plants had lengthened into a stem and were even putting forth a second whorl of leaves, and all the slope that had seemed so recently a lifeless stretch of litter was now dark with the stunted olive-green herbage of bristling spikes that swayed with the vigour of their growing.

It's possible that Wells might have read earlier comments similar to those given by Professor Pickering about the possibility of vegetation upon the lunar surface. It is probably unlikely that Wells' novel was the basis for Pickering's ideas about lunar foliage. Undoubtedly, he simply misinterpreted the shadows and other visual anomalies that he observed in the photographic plates made of the crater Eratosthenes.

Although in the end, the announcement of life on the lunar surface was not correct, it did cause quite a stir for a time in the early 1920s. Since then, a number of UFO researchers have posited that although the moon is essentially a dead world, the lunar surface may have been visited by extraterrestrials at some point in our planet's past and that perhaps the moon was used as a base of operations, from which the ETs launched surveillance missions to study the Earth?

Close up of the Lunar Crater Eratosthenes (NASA)

11

MOTHMAN IN NEBRASKA?

Hubbell, Nebraska
February 22, 1922

WE, THE AUTHORS, always strive to report on the cases with the strongest documentation, serving to bolster their truthfulness. We avoid stories that do not have a lot of supporting documentation – with only a few exceptions, such as the case that follows. The story of a UFO sighting and the appearance of an unearthly creature in 1922 is so intriguing that we felt compelled to include it here, although we tell our readers from the start that it lacks the clear support that most of our other stories have.

The story originates from highly respected UFO researcher Jacques Vallée, who said that he first read the story in a letter from the eyewitness, William C. Lamb. Vallée said he found the letter while looking through the "UFO files" at the U.S. Air Force's Aerospace Technical Intelligence Center at Wright-Patterson Air Base in Dayton, Ohio, in the 1950s or 1960s. The original letter has apparently been lost over time; however, and Vallée has published a summary of its contents in several books over the years, including *Passport of Magonia: A Century of Landings* and *Anatomy of a Phenomenon.*

Vallée (left) with J. Allen Hynek, Circa 1977 (U.S. Government Photo)

According to the story, on February 22, 1922, at 5 a.m., the witness, William C. Lamb, was out hunting in the snowy woods near Hubbell,

Nebraska, when he encountered some strange tracks in the snow that he subsequently followed, trying to determine what type of creature might have made them. As Lamb moved farther into the woods, Lamb suddenly heard a high-pitched "shrieking" sound that was seemingly coming from the sky above him.

Looking up, he saw a dark, circular or spherical object flying overhead, which, as it passed, hid the stars in the sky above. Frightened by the apparition, Lamb hid behind a tree as he noticed that the "brilliantly lighted" UFO descended out of the sky and moved closer to his position.

The strange craft landed in a hollow or depression nearby. Moments later, from the area where the ship had landed, which was about 65 feet from where Lamb stood, there came a bizarre flying creature, about 8 feet in length, that flew right past Lamb's hiding place.

At some point, the beast, described as a "magnificent flying creature" was said to have landed "like an aircraft" and began walking in the snow, leaving behind a trail of strange tracks. The stunned hunter followed the tracks left by the creature for about five miles before he gave up his search.

Some researchers have compared this incident to the reports in the 1960s of a strange, winged creature that came to be known as "Mothman." This bizarre flying beast was sighted in several places in and around Point Pleasant, West Virginia. The West Virginia Mothman sightings became the basis for several books and a 2002 major motion picture titled *The Mothman Prophecies.*

Initial descriptions of the creature stated it was a large gray humanoid whose eyes glowed red when car headlights shown upon it. Witnesses said it looked like a "large flying man with ten-foot wings." Others described it as "a large bird with red eyes." The sightings remain a mystery today, despite a number of attempts by scientists to say that what witnesses saw was a large sandhill crane, which has a seven-foot wingspan and reddish coloration around its eyes. This attempt at an explanation was not universally accepted.

Artist's Depiction of Mothman
By Tim Bertelink - Own work, CC BY-SA 4.0,

https://commons.wikimedia.org/w/index.php?curid=46584699

An account of the Hubbell, Nebraska incident in 1922 is said to have appeared in the Lincoln, Nebraska, local newspaper the *Daily Star*, although the exact date of the article is unknown, and the authors of this book were unable to locate it. The late Gray Baker (1925 - 1984), a UFO researcher, said he found the newspaper article, which reported that a spherical object landed near the witness's house, after which an eight-foot-tall creature emerged that the witness described as looking like "the devil."

In another version of this incident, paranormal researcher Albert Rosales states that the eyewitness, Lamb, who was a "deeply religious man," said the creature looked so much like the devil that he shouted out "Get thee behind me, Satan" and turned his back to the monster.

Rosales also claims that the witness provided a number of other details that were clearly based on a religious interpretation of what was happening to him, such as that the creature's tracks in the snow resembled hoof marks.

Whether the hunter sighted a devilish alien or bore witness to Mothman's very first appearance on Earth, it is certainly a curious encounter to say the least.

Giant Meteor Startles New Jersey Coast Towns

ASBURY PARK, N. J., April 24.— A meteor discharging odorous gases passed south of here with a thunderous roar at 9 o'clock last night and frightened residents of many coast towns. Window panes in homes in Toms River were shattered by the explosion and the gases, polluting the atmosphere for more than a quarter of an hour, compelled the residents to hold dampened handkerchiefs to their nostrils. At Lakehurst many buildings were shaken.

The phenomenon lasted about a minute. A tiny streak of light at first, it became beautifully colored as it neared the earth and at times appeared to halt momentarily in space, adopt a new course, then zig-zag back again, witnesses said.

The meteor fell into the sea about a mile off shore at Seaside park, thirty-five miles south of here. The celestial mass as it struck the water caused an explosion that shook the village and threw spray to a great hight. Volumes of steam then arose and drifting ashore, nauseated many.

Indianapolis News April 24, 1922 p.6

12

MASSIVE "METEOR" SPLASHES DOWN OFF JERSEY COAST

Toms River, New Jersey
April 24, 1922

THOUGH THIS CASE is classified by many scientists today as an unusual meteor crash, the devil is in the details they say. On April 24, 1922, a huge heavenly body crashed down into the waters off the coast of New Jersey. The *Indianapolis News* reported that, "A meteor discharging odorous gasses passed south of here with a thunderous roar at 9 o'clock last night and frightened residents of many coast towns. Window panes in homes in

Toms River were shattered by the explosion and the gases, polluting the atmosphere for more than a quarter of an hour, compelled the residents to hold dampened handkerchiefs to their nostrils. At Lakehurst many buildings were shaken."

ALONG THE RIVER. PINE BEACH. N. J.

Postcard Depicting 1920's era scene near Toms River, N.J.

The nauseating odor itself isn't totally unusual for a meteor. Some meteors are known to smell like sulfur. Horrible odors are not uncommon when dealing with UFO sightings as well. Witnesses to a UFO landing in Braxton County, West Virginia, in the early 1950s reported on a horrendous odor in association with the craft and the alien being they saw.

Though it's an interesting detail, the smell isn't what made this incident so unusual. It was the behavior of the "meteor." The article's second paragraph is certainly illuminating in more ways than one: "The phenomenon lasted about a minute. A tiny streak of light at first, it became beautifully colored as it neared the earth and at times appeared to halt momentarily in space, adopt a new course, then zig zag back again, witnesses said."

FUMES

Are Spread By Meteor

In New Jersey Town—Explosion Breaks Windows When Mass Plunges Into Sea.

Article appearing in The Cincinnati Enquirer, April 24, 1922, p.1

Meteors, as we have said so many times before, do not change their course or their speed. The witnesses claiming that the heavenly body was "zig zagging" and changing speed is the smoking gun proving that this was not a meteor, but some sort of craft.

The article concluded: "The meteor fell into the sea about a mile off shore at Seaside Park, thirty-five miles south of here. The celestial mass as it struck the water caused an explosion that shook the village and threw spray to a great hight [sic]. Volumes of steam then arose and drifting ashore, nauseated many."

More interesting is the conclusion of a separate article published in The *Cincinnati Enquirer* on the same day. Their article ended with the following: "Members of two Coast Guard companies said they believed the occurrence had been caused by a large explosive rocket."

For the record, there was no rocket powerful enough in 1922 to cause the damage that the so-called meteor did when it plunged into the water.

Nor does the strangeness stop there. The area in which this meteor fell was no stranger to strangeness. Preceding its arrival was the infamous Jersey Devil, a winged horse-like entity. In the 1930s, neighboring areas would be subject to more aerial anomalies. On December 5, 1931, in Folsom Swamp, Atlantic County, New Jersey, many people reported seeing a pilot parachuting out of what appeared to be a burning aircraft. There would also be a UFO incident at Beach Haven in 1933. Odder yet, many years later, also in the month of April, another meteor plunged into Barnegat Bay, located only five miles from the Toms River incident. The incident occurred on April 18, 1979. April showers indeed...

13

FALLEN UFO?

Blackstone, Virginia
May 11, 1922

WHEN A HUGE object, estimated at twenty tons, smashed into the ground near Blackstone, Virginia, on May 11, 1922, at 11:15 p.m., the conventional wisdom was that it was a "giant meteor." The incident was significant for the purposes of this book because of several reported paranormal events associated with the fall of this object.

The May 13, 1922, edition of *The News and Observer* in Raleigh, North Carolina, said, "The shock of a twenty-ton meteor which crashed to the ground in an isolated spot in Nottoway County, 12 miles northwest of Blackstone, late last night, was felt for a radius of fifty miles, while the brilliant glare of the incandescent body illuminated the heavens over southern Virginia and sections of North Carolina."

SHOCK OF GIANT METEOR IS FELT OVER WIDE AREA

ASSOCIATED PRESS MAN IN RALEIGH SCOOPS THE WORLD ON METEOR STORY

Robin O. King, Jr., who has charge of the Associated Press news bureau in Raleigh, was the first newspaper man to spot the big meteor that caused such a commotion in Old Virginia Thursday night. King had started home when he saw the meteor high up

Twenty-Ton Bolide Crashes To The Ground In An Isolated Spot In Nottoway County, Virginia

MAKES HOLE IN EARTH WITH AN AREA OF FIVE HUNDRED SQUARE FEET

The News and Observer (Raleigh, N.C.),
May 13, 1922, p. 1

The report went on to say that the meteor was composed of a metallic substance and that it crashed into a grove of oak trees with an explosive roar, creating a 500-square-foot pit. "Flames which immediately shot up were visible for many miles, while trees caught fire," the newspaper report said. Residents in the vicinity of the impact site felt the ground shake as if in an earthquake.

"In Norfolk [Virginia], the meteor appeared to be about half the diameter of the full moon and much like a street arc-light. Its tail, of orange brilliance with a sharp blue flame fading out at the extreme end, apparently was about ten or twelve

Charles Pollard Olivier
(1884-1975)

times as long and fully as broad as the body.... The entire southwestern skies were illuminated as if by a flash of lighting and a burst of flames," the article said.

The velocity of the object was later calculated by astronomer Charles Pollard Olivier to be about 59 kilometers per second, which equates to about 37 miles per second. Olivier wrote an article titled "The Great Meteor of May 11, 1922" for the magazine *Popular Astronomy* (1925, Vol. 33), in which he said, "A great fireball or meteor appeared over North Carolina, and travelling northward, burst over Amelia County, Virginia. The writer's attention was called to this meteor by sensational notices that appeared in the daily papers during the next few days. From these it was evident that the reports must have referred to a remarkable phenomenon, hence efforts were made to secure authentic data."

After an event of this magnitude, surely the crash site would yield a wealth of physical evidence, right? Actually, it did not. As was reported in *The News Reporter* (Littleton, N.C.), "As far as we can determine, the meteor appears to have been lost.... One theory is that the meteor was of some combustible material or chemical, and when it struck the earth, exploded and disappeared."

Another newspaper, *The Reidsville (N. C.) Review* of May 23, 1922, said, "The whole section which was shaken by the explosion following the meteor's fall has been combed but there is no sign of the astral visitor. The belief now prevails that the meteor was surcharged with gases which blew the meteor to particles so minute that there is no trace of it. Reports that a large pit was formed in the earth have proved totally erroneous, this proving to be a depression in the earth in Nottoway which existed long before the meteor came."

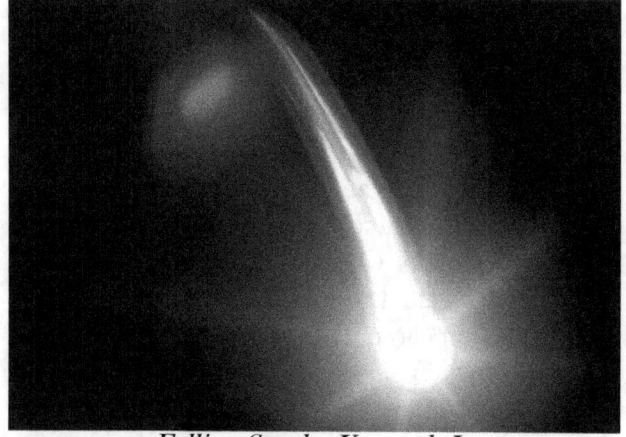

Falling Star by Kenneth Lu

As previously mentioned, the fall of this "meteor" led to a number of reported paranormal events, as noted by researcher Chris Aubeck in his 2015 book *Return to Magonia*. One of the most notable appeared in an article in the *Greensboro (N. C.) Daily News* of May 22, 1922, which told the story of a group of eight people from Greensboro who drove to the site of the meteor crash and heard something that was extremely strange.

A party composed of Mr. and Mrs. W. L. Thomas, Charles, Walter L. and Edmund Thomas, Misses Graves and Ella Satterfield and Taylor Long left here in automobiles early last Sunday morning for Blackstone to see the fallen meteor, but returned, however, stating that the nearer the locality, that had been described by the press, that the meteor fell they found upon inquiring of the neighborhood people that they knew nothing of the event and they returned home without ever locating the much talked-of area. It is reported by others who claim to have been and seen that more strange than the meteor itself is an old man of unearthly appearance who stands near the scene immobile, neither speaking or apparently looking at the throngs of curious sightseers. The superstitious believing that he came down with the precipitating meteor.

Greensboro (North Carolina) Daily News,
May 22, 1922, p. 5

The excursionists left early on Sunday, May 21, and headed for Blackstone, Virginia, the town nearest to the fallen meteor. Upon arriving in the area, though, they found that none of the local residents knew the exact location of the meteor crash site. However, they did have a very unusual story to tell. The article said, "It is reported by others who claim to have been near, that stranger than the meteor itself, is an old man of unearthly appearance who stood near the scene immobile, neither speaking nor apparently looking at the throngs of curious sightseers. The superstitious believing that he came down with the precipitating meteor."

Was the "old man of unearthly appearance" an alien being, or was he perhaps just a ghost, thus making this another strange example of how sometimes more than one type of phenomenon can manifest in one area?

THE GREAT METEOR OF MAY 11, 1922.

By CHAS. P. OLIVIER.

On the night of May 11, 1922, at 11ʰ 15ᵐ E. S. T., a great fireball or meteor appeared over North Carolina, and travelling northward, burst over Amelia County, Virginia. The writer's attention was called to this meteor by sensational notices that appeared in the daily papers during the next few days. From these it was evident that the reports must have referred to a remarkable phenomenon, hence efforts were made to secure authentic data.

On behalf of the American Meteor Society, large numbers of standard questionnaires were mailed to high school superintendents, postmasters and certain other persons. In addition large numbers of personal letters were written, following up the return of the question-

---

Popular Astronomy, 1925, Vol. 33, p. 502

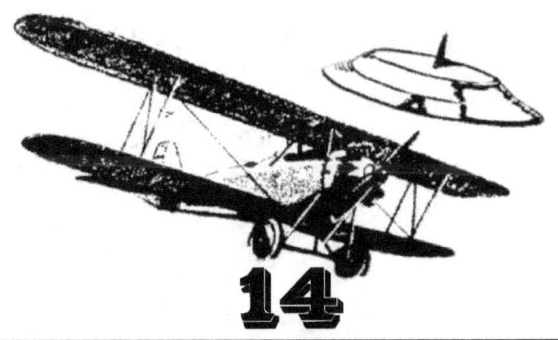

14
ENCOUNTER WITH UFO ENTITIES

Detroit, Michigan
Summer 1922

IN EARLY 1978, Irma Jean Hinz of Wayne, Michigan, contacted Dr. Ron Westrum, professor of sociology and consultant for the Mutual UFO Network (MUFON) about a remarkable UFO encounter she had as a teenager in the summer of 1922 in Detroit.

Irma was 15 years old in 1922 and had gone out on a date to see a movie with a young man named William O' Brien. After the movie, at about 10 p.m., the young couple was walking back toward Irma's house when they had their incredible encounter. It happened as they walked south along South Dragoon Street near the intersection of

West Jefferson Avenue, in the area of Fort Wayne, a few blocks north of the Detroit River.

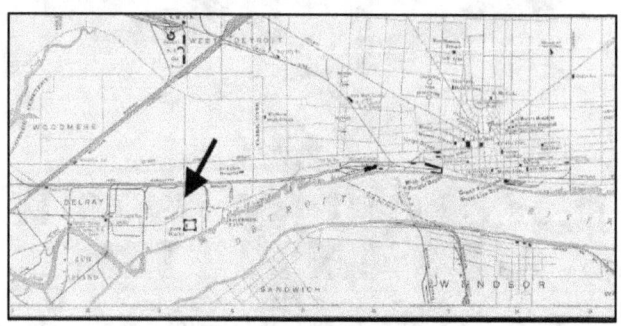

1924 Map of Detroit, Showing the Site of the Encounter

The strange encounter began with a sudden bright illumination that lit up the area all around them. This was followed by the appearance of a most remarkable object. Descending from the sky in front of them was a large, disk-shaped object, hovering over a vacant lot at about the height of a large tree. The disk-shaped craft slowly revolved as it hovered, and the witnesses noticed a row of rectangular windows, lit from within, around the perimeter of the bottom of the object.

As amazing as this sight was to the teenage observers, what they saw next was even more startling to them. Looking into the windows near the bottom of the craft, they saw approximately 20 humanoid beings that seemed to be staring intently at them.

The strange beings, which could only be seen from their shoulders up, were bald-headed with eyes set close together. Irma could not remember any other distinguishing features of the creatures. She and her companion continued looking at the remarkable sight for several minutes.

Artist's Depiction of UFO

Concerned that the humanoids were watching them so closely and worried what the beings' intent might be, Irma and her date became frightened and began to quickly move away from the area.

After arriving back at her home, Irma Hinz told her parents about the encounter, and she said that they believed her. After keeping the story to herself for many years, Irma decided to make it public in 1978 and filed a formal sighting report with MUFON's Ted Bloecher on August 27, 1978.

Irma passed away in her hometown of Wayne, Michigan, on March 27, 1999, at the age of 92.

Dateline: U.S. Forces

ROCHELLE— U.S. Air Force CPT Jerry N. Massie, son of Mr. and Mrs. Norman W. Massie, Fairfield, has received his M.S. degree at the Air Force Institute of Technology (AFIT), Wright-Patterson AFB, Ohio.

AFIT provides accredited graduate-level resident education for selected military and key government employes in scientific, technological and other fields.

Capt Massie, who majored in logistics management, has been reassigned to Headquarters, Military Airlift Command at Scott AFB.

A 1959 graduate of Fairfield Community High School, he received his B.A. degree in political science from Southern Illinois University in 1964 and was commissioned the following year upon completion of Officer Training School at Lackland AFB, Tex. The captain's wife, Marcia, is the daughter of Mr. and Mrs. F. William Eber, 426 N. 11th St.

Dixon (Illinois) Evening Telegraph
Sep. 21, 1971, p. 9

15

MOUNT ERIE'S EERIE UFO ENCOUNTER

Mount Erie, Illinois
June 1923

✝

IN A DECEMBER 27, 2019 article titled "Evansville-area man once had a chilling close encounter with a UFO," reporter Jon Webb, of the *Evansville (Illinois) Courier & Press,* told the incredible story of an up close UFO encounter experienced by Norman Massie, a native of Mount Erie, Illinois. Massie's story had also been told in an August 12, 1998 *Courier & Press* article by Len Wells titled "Close Encounter."

Massie, a long-time Southern Illinois teacher and basketball coach, worked in Wayne County, Illinois, schools for almost 40 years. According to

Webb, he also "sold World Book Encyclopedias on the side, schlepping hardbound volumes to knowledge-hungry residents all over the Tri-State."

Artist's Rendition of UFO

One morning in June 1923, Massie, age 10, was leading the family horses into the pasture when he saw something incredible. "I opened the gate to let the horses into the pasture. I let them through, and as I was closing the gate, I looked back down the field and there was an object with lights all around it."

Rather than being frightened, the boy was intensely curious. "The machine was metallic and stood on three legs. The top was a dome with holes in it. The best way I could describe the top was it looked like melted glass."

Massie found himself moving closer to the object, approaching to within 50 feet when he realized that the craft had a crew inside it. "I kept walking closer to the object until I got about 50 feet away. I stood there and watched the five men who were on board."

Massie described the men as being about four and a half feet tall with blond hair. "I got close enough that I could hear them talk," Massie said. "One guy sat in a chair and the others called him the commander. Four others made trips back and forth in the ship. I didn't know what was going on until the end."

Interestingly, Massie seemed to hear the crew's conversation as if it were spoken in English, although he might have intercepted their thoughts rather than hearing their speech.

Also fascinating is that, although the humanoids were short in stature which fits the description of many other UFO occupants, Massie described them as having blond hair, which is unusual in UFO lore.

Massie also said he heard one of the crew members tell the "commander" that "the repairs had been made." At this point, the sighting had lasted about five minutes, and it became obvious to Massie that, with repairs completed, the strange object was about to depart.

"In a minute, it came to a hovering position. The tripod legs telescoped up into the belly of the thing, and it went straight up about 200 feet and whizzed off to the west like a bullet."

Confused and startled, Massie ran home and told his parents, Grover and Laura Massie, and his 8-year-old brother, Lyveere. "Mom and Dad tried to convince me that I really hadn't seen anything and was making up the whole thing." His dad announced to the family that he wanted no one mentioning the incident to anyone because they might think Norman was "crazy in the head, or an idiot."

Massie kept his silence for 67 years, until 1990. While talking to his son Jerry, who had risen in rank to colonel in the U.S. Air Force, he disclosed the story of what happened for the first time. Ironically, Jerry had earlier studied at Wright-Patterson Air Force Base in Ohio, which has a long history with UFO lore.

Massie said, "When I got done telling him the whole story, he told me there was nothing wrong with me, that the Air Force files are full of pictures of UFOs. He accepted my story as the truth."

According to Len Wells, Massie was convinced the object had to come from somewhere other than Earth. Massie said, "It doesn't bother me one bit that people might think I'm a crazy old man. In my own mind and my own heart, it existed, and I saw it with my own two eyes.

Massie stated that although the encounter lasted no more than five minutes, it "haunted" him for the rest of his life. On the occasion of Massie's death in 2004 at the age of 91, Len Wells, the reporter who originally interviewed him, wrote that Massie's UFO story was extremely convincing because he was not the kind of person who would make things up. Wells wrote, "I've heard Norman tell this story many times, and it was always the same. Never embellished from one time to the next."

Wells concluded by saying, "His story has traveled around the globe and is still shared by those who remain convinced we've received visitors from other planets."

16

REVOLVING RED UFO

Greencastle, Indiana
1923

✴

IN 1923, TWO COLLEGE students at DePauw University in Greencastle, Indiana, had an amazing UFO sighting that they waited decades before disclosing. The students were Herrick Greenleaf, 29, and Andrew Wallace Crandall, 28, who remained lifelong friends and both became professors at DePauw.

The students saw an enormous object, round in shape and glowing brightly, approach a highway at low altitude. The young men were driving west at about 9 p.m., Crandall and Greenleaf, sighted the object near the intersection of U.S. Highway 40 and Indiana Highway 100, just east of Indianapolis.

They stated that the object was as large as a modern passenger plane.

Artist's Conception by SoundTrackUniverse from Pixabay

The UFO first appeared from out of the northeast, gliding to stop parallel with the road surface at an altitude of about 500 feet. The witnesses stated that it loomed over the area, casting an incredibly brilliant red light upon all the surrounding countryside.

According to Gordon Lore and Harold Deneault, in their 1968 book *Mysteries of the Skies: UFOs in Perspective*: "The UFO cut diagonally across their path. Its size was breathtaking... The gigantic 'saucer' was revolving! The scene was made more unnatural by the deep silence, as the machine spun noiselessly through the night."

The strange craft suddenly vanished "as if the light had been turned off." The witnesses could not discern whether the object zoomed off at an incredibly high rate of speed or if it just vanished in thin air.

"As if the light had been turned off," one professor later said, "the disc vanished!"

Somewhere in the southwest, not too distant from the observers, it had simply disappeared, giving not the slightest hint how this feat was accomplished. Whether the UFO had bolted off at thousands of miles per hour, or whether it had winked out to become invisible, remains a mystery.

The round, glowing object moved silently from northeast to southwest, and then vanished. The incident was reported in the 1968 book *Mysteries of the Skies: UFOs in Perspective*, by Gordon Lore and Harold Deneault.

The students' story becomes especially significant when one considers that witness Herrick Greenleaf later became a professor of astronomy and mathematics at DePauw University, serving in that role for 39 years, retiring in 1961.

Herrick Greenleaf (middle) - DePauw University Photo

Additionally, Greenleaf served in World War I. His friend Andrew Wallace Crandall became a recognized professor in Depauw's history department. He was an authority on the American Civil War and also served 39 years, retiring along with Greenleaf.

Greenleaf passed away in 1979 at age 84, and Crandall died in 1963 at age 68.

Andrew Crandall in Later Years (DePauw Photo)

17

HUMANOIDS IN ROBES

Mount Desert Island, Maine
Autumn 1923

AUTHOR AND UFO researcher Raymond E. Fowler told a story of a very unusual incident that happened to his father in 1923, while his dad was stationed at the U. S. Navy Radio Compass Station at Otter Cliffs on Mount Desert Island, Maine. Fowler's story appeared in in his 2004 book *Synchrofile: Amazing Personal Encounters with Synchronicity and Other Strange Phenomena.*

Using a tape recorder, Raymond Fowler taped his father's story and later transcribed it for his book. The elder Fowler started his story by saying that he was 22 years old and was a radioman in charge of the naval station. His shift was from 4 p.m. to 4 a.m.

Otter Cliffs, Acadia National Park,
Bar Harbor, Mt. Desert Island, Me.

Postcard Circa 1930 (Public Domain)

"One late autumn day, a violent electrical storm was in progress when I reached the station to relieve the day man. He left for the main transatlantic station a quarter of a mile away wishing me luck. I would need it, for static was terrific. The storm winds were near hurricane strength and had spread out over the North Atlantic shipping lanes. The ships were constantly calling in for bearings."

Although the exact date is not given, this may have occurred during one of several storms that affected the area in the autumn of 1923, including a strong offshore disturbance during the last week of October.

At 11 p.m., the elder Fowler was responding to a request for bearings from the ocean liner *S.S. George Washington*, when a violent lightning bolt hit the radio cable outside the naval station and, seeking ground, the strong electrical charge travelled into the building, striking Fowler in his torso.

*The S.S. George Washington
During World War I*

"It lodged behind my solar plexus where it remained and revolved like a fiery sun inside of me," the radioman said, "By this time, I should be dead, I thought."

What happened next was beyond belief. He saw a "soft light" move apparently from his body up through the roof and out into the night, moving toward what appeared to be "a radiant star." Other "rays of light" seemed to come from him and expand about seven feet around him in all directions.

Raymond E. Fowler
(Courtesy Jerry Pippin)

"Three distinct flashes of light unfolded into three majestic-looking smiling men in shining robes of light. Although they did not speak, my thoughts and theirs were in perfect attunement, making verbal speech unnecessary. My thoughts formed many questions concerning them: the light rays, the electronic fire inside of me, and what manner of star it was that projected such rays," Fowler said.

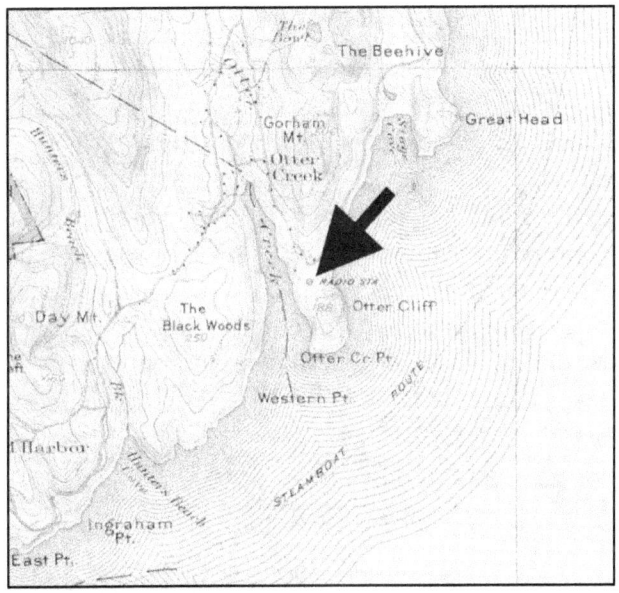

1922 Map of Maine Showing Location of Incident

"These three beings were fine-featured and had light cream-textured complexions. Their eyes were so bright, it was difficult to see their color, but I thought they were blue. The brilliant aura surrounding them made it impossible for me to determine the color of their hair, for they wore strange velvety-looking hats that were like three tiers of rolls upon their heads. Like their robes, the headdresses were rich blue in color. They wore soft doe-skin-like form-fitting boots."

The being to the left of Fowler pointed his finger at the fiery ball of light on Fowler's abdomen and in a flash of light, it leaped into the being's hand. The humanoid then tossed it to the being next to him, and it tossed it to the third being in turn, who threw it into the copper mesh screening of the station. The fiery ball went up in a shower of sparks and disappeared. All three men then smiled, bowed again, and disappeared in three flashes of light.

According to Raymond Fowler, this incident troubled his father for the rest of his life. "This experience was etched in Dad's memory and each time he told it to us from childhood to adulthood, the details never varied," Raymond Fowler said.

18

UFO LIGHT SHOW

Benton, Illinois
1923

IN 1923, THE CHILDREN of a family living in Benton, Illinois, were out playing in their front yard after supper when they had an incredible UFO encounter with an object that was equipped with a number of interesting, multicolored lights.

Several years after the event, one of the eyewitnesses told the tale, "One evening after supper, we went out in front of our house to play, when we noticed something like a small cloud in the cloudless sky."

It seemed unusual that the approaching "cloud" was the only feature of an otherwise perfectly clear evening sky. But even more unusual was the fact that the strange cloud was drawing closer by the minute.

Noticing that the cloud was approaching, the witness told the other children, "There's something in the sky."

The object was advancing from the north and was not very high in the sky, according to the witness. It began to slow down as it approached the area near where the children were playing.

Having slowed down and descended even further, the object flew past the fairground and near a school. "It slowed down like a top and flew low around the old fairground. [It] then came back by the Grant School west to the electrical poles, stopping before crossing the railroad tracks."

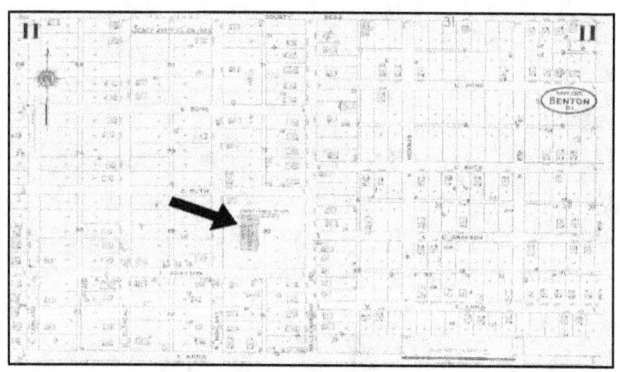

1925 Street Map of Benton, Illinois, Showing Grant School

The object was now as low as the nearby treetops. Suddenly, the children saw a row of multicolored lights come on near the bottom of the craft. "The lights came on around the bottom edge—red, blue, green and ecru [beige]. The ecru light or spotlight was very bright."

Image by PhotoVision from Pixabay

The children watched the UFO light show in fascination for "a few minutes." Then suddenly, the main light on the ship was turned off, and the object seemed to move closer to a nearby line of electrical poles.

What happened next was quite unexpected. The object rose up high in the sky, apparently ready to depart the area, but then began descending slowly until it landed just beyond the railroad tracks. As it was about to land, the bottom of the craft "moved" and four flood lights suddenly turned on, causing a "pillar of light."

"I looked away for a minute, and when I looked back it was gone," the witness added.

The story was not made public for many years, according to the witness. "It was years before I saw a picture of a UFO, and then I knew the mystery object I had seen was a UFO."

This story appeared in Philip L. Rife's 2001 book titled *It Didn't Start with Roswell: 50 Years of Amazing UFO Crashes, Close Encounters and Coverups*, on page 96.

19

TINY ROBOTS

Dade City, Florida
1924

IN HIS 2001 BOOK, *It Didn't Start with Roswell,*
UFO researcher Philip Rife recounted the amazing
story of a young girl who had a startling UFO
encounter in the playground of her Catholic grade
school in South Florida in 1924. The incident was
first reported by the eyewitness, Evelyn Wendt,
fifty years after it happened in a 1974 article
published in a West Palm Beach, Florida, weekly
newspaper called *The Weekday.*

According to Wendt, she was in the playground
of the Holy Name Convent School in Pasco
County, back in 1924, when she suddenly noticed
an egg-shaped "saucer" on the ground. The object
at first emitted a bright light, which Wendt said was
shining in her eyes.

Saint Leo Abbey in Pasco County
(Public Domain)

Then the light went out and a "hatch" opened on the object, out of which came some very strange tiny creatures that the witness later referred to as "robot people." In her account of the incident, she stated, "They were smaller than I and resembled animated flowers with faces where the bud would be. Remember, I was just a bitty thing then, and kids don't fear flowers."

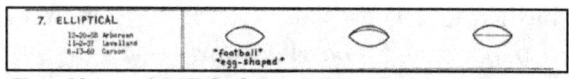

Egg-Shaped UFO from NICAP Chart (1964)

In addition to these tiny, flower-like "robots," a normal-sized humanoid appeared alongside them. Both the humanoid and the strange little creatures started moving toward the school, in the direction of the "science building." They carried with them a strange device that she understood to be a weapon of some kind. She tried to help them carry the device, but it was too heavy for her, and she got the impression that they did not want her to assist them.

Artist's Conception of UFO

Although Wendt heard no talking among the visitors, she seemed to be able to understand their thoughts. They communicated to her that their mission was to go into the science building and put a stop to work that was going on inside. They told her that if they did not put a stop to it, the building and possibly the surrounding area would soon be destroyed.

Wendt said that a short time later the strange visitors came back out of the science building, having completed their task and having left the science building "in shambles."

As the strange humanoid and tiny robots were about to board their ship, one of the strangers asked her if she wanted to go with them. She answered no. Afterward, the creatures told her that they would come back for her in 35 years, but as of 1974, they had not returned.

After entering their ship, the "saucer" flew straight up into the air and hovered for a minute before completely disappearing.

According to author Rife, this amazing story first appeared in Timothy G. Beckley's 1981 book titled *Timothy G. Beckley's Book of Space Contacts.* The eyewitness account is still not widely known among UFO researchers.

20

THE COWBOYS SAW A UFO

Osage Hills, Oklahoma
January 1924

IN JANUARY 1924, 18-year-old Perry Guy Powers, a native of Kansas, was working at a ranch in the rugged Osage Hills of Oklahoma when he and another ranch hand had an incredible UFO sighting.

The two cowboys were on horseback at 1 a.m., returning to their ranch, when they observed a beam of light shining down from the sky onto the snow between their two horses.

Turning their gaze upwards, they traced the beam of light up into the sky, where the men saw that it emanated from a large, oval-shaped UFO that was moving across the sky above them. "It was as large as a silver dollar held at arm's length," Powers said,

"[It] crossed from horizon to horizon in less than three minutes."

Cowboy Rider (Photo by Jean Beufort)

The object's hull was peppered by white dots of light along its side – perhaps portholes. At the trailing end, the object emitted a blue flame.

As the cowboys watched the object passing overhead, the only sound detectable was a slight hissing noise coming from the craft. Eventually, it disappeared beyond the horizon.

Powers kept his experience hidden for 30 years until 1954, when his story appeared in *Civilian Saucer Investigation Quarterly Bulletin*, dated Winter 1954. The publication was from the independent UFO research group called Civilian Saucer Intelligence (CSI), which existed from 1954 until 1959 and whose founders included highly regarded UFO researcher Ted Bloecher.

Between the time of his sighting (1924) and its disclosure thirty years later, Powers worked as a roper and gave exhibitions of his bullwhip skills –

at one point working with Gene Autry at Madison Square Garden. He also worked at breaking and training horses for celebrities, including Autry, Bing Crosby, and Nevada politician Pat McKarran, after whom the Las Vegas Airport is named.

Image by d0ran from Pixabay

Powers served in World War II in the Marine Corps and also served at one point on the Battleship Missouri.

According to a copy of the eulogy delivered at his funeral, which is posted on *WikiTree.com,* Warner Brothers once offered Powers a leading role in the 1952 movie *The Story of Will Rogers*, but he declined due to being employed in the defense industry. He worked for aircraft defense contractor Lockheed, in Burbank, California, from 1952 until 1974, when he retired due to failing health.

In the eulogy, a friend described Powers as a gentle, soft-spoken man who loved all people and tried very hard to get along with everyone. "If everyone were like him, the world would be a much better place in which to live," said his eulogist.

Historical documents indicate that Powers was born on July 3, 1906, in La Harpe, Kansas. He died on June 8, 1981, in Santa Clara, California, at age 75. The 1940 U.S. Census lists his occupation as "Ranch Hand" and his Industry as "Dude Ranches."

So, not only was the witness in this encounter a very real person, he was also highly respected and very credible. In the absence of physical evidence of extraterrestrials, a sound witness usually makes for the foundation of a legitimate UFO sighting.

21
MEN IN BLACK IN BRAXTON COUNTY

Gem, West Virginia
May 1924

✈

IN WRITING THESE BOOKS, we have been amazed to learn that famous UFO "hotspots" of the 20th century are the very places where unusual incidents happened in the past as well. For example, 100 years before Calvin Parker and Charles Hickson were abducted by aliens in Pascagoula, Mississippi, in 1973, a strange UFO passed over the abduction sight in 1874. No ordinary UFO sighting, the object was described as a giant, luminous cloud travelling under its own power and exuding so much heat that people literally feared that their homes would burst into flame and that the hair on their heads would be singed off.

Similarly, in the same area where a UFO crash is said to have occurred in 1965, another significant UFO sighting took place way back in 1829. Could it be that certain geographical areas tend to attract these paranormal events?

In yet another unusual "coincidence," a UFO sighting in 1924 happened in the same place where the famous "Flatwoods Monster" incident occurred three decades later – Braxton County, West Virginia.

On September 12, 1952, three boys – brothers Edward and Fred May and their friend Tommy Hyer – saw a strange, brightly-lit object land on the property of a local farmer. The boys ran and told their mother, Kathleen May. The mother, her boys, and Tommy then decided to trek to the spot where they felt the craft landed. Along the way, they were joined by local children Neil Nunley and Ronnie Shaver, and a West Virginia National Guardsman named Eugene Lemon. The group of eyewitnesses was large and very diverse.

What the group encountered sounded like something out of a horror movie. Where the object landed, they saw a ten-foot-tall creature that defies description. It was, for lack of a better word, truly alien. The head was red and shaped like an "ace of spades," while the eyes were a greenish orange. It had small, claw-like hands and seemed to levitate and glide rather than walk. In more recent years, ufologists have speculated that the creature might have been an android rather than a living being.

Needless to say, the witnesses ran away in sheer terror, and their sighting became a media sensation. Due to the large group of witnesses, the case was taken very seriously.

Eugene Lemon (left) and Kathleen May (right) pose with an artist's rendition of the creature. AP Photo.

Twenty-eight years earlier, another very unusual event took place in the same area of the Flatwoods Monster sighting. Author Phillip Rife, in his book *It Didn't Start with Roswell*, tells an amazing tale of the reported crash of a UFO near the small West Virginia town of Gem in May 1924. The story was originally researched by legendary paranormal author John A. Keel, who was one of the first researcher to write extensively about the strange "Men in Black" —mysterious individuals that appear after a UFO incident and attempt to intimidate and silence the witnesses.

Residents of the town witnessed an object that was "as big as a battleship" flying erratically overhead and plunging down from the sky in the thick woods outside the town. A party of men, including the local sheriff and a local resident named John Cole, systematically searched the woods. Within hours, they found the wreck in a small clearing.

"It didn't look like much of a flying machine," said Cole. "In fact, it was a wonder it could fly at all. It was like the fuselage of a modern plane, with windows and all. But it didn't have any wings, tail, or propellers."

UFO Crash Diorama (Photo by Noe Torres)

The witness continued, "It was mighty big. I'd say at least 75 feet long. It filled the whole clearing."

But the most surprising thing about the crash site was that there were "five or six men" surrounding the crashed object, all of them dressed in very peculiar clothing. "We weren't the first ones there, though. There were already five or six men in the clearing. Some of them were dressed in black business suits, neckties and all, and that seemed damned silly in that neck of the woods," the witness said.

Artist's Rendition of Men in Black
by RadioKirk - Vectorised by MesserWoland
(CC BY-SA (http://creativecommons.org/licenses/by-sa/3.0/)

Interestingly, these men in black suits and neckties fit the description of the so-called "Men in Black," which started appearing widely in the 1950s after UFO incidents had occurred. As we have previously pointed out in this book series, there were several "Men in Black" sightings in the 1800s and early 1900s, long before anyone knew what to call them.

The strangers were all small in stature, about five feet tall, and they all looked "Oriental," with high cheekbones, slanted eyes, and dark skin. These, too, are common features attributed to the Men in Black. For instance, in 1897, Judge Lawrence A. Byrne encountered Men in Black with Asian features piloting an airship in McKinney Bayou, Arkansas. There were other cases, but notably an Asian man dressed in all black also interviewed people about UFOs in Point Pleasant, West Virginia, during the Mothman sightings of the 1960s.

But back to our 1924 sighting in Gem, West Virginia. Along with the dark-suited strangers were others that were dressed in coveralls of a funny color, made of a very shiny material.

The strangers were talking among themselves in a language that none of the townspeople could identify. When the strange group saw the townspeople approaching, they got "real excited," and the ones dressed in coveralls ran inside the crashed airship, as if they were trying to hide from the newcomers.

Some of the townspeople were armed with guns, and one of them, disturbed by the bizarre appearance and behavior of the strangers, raised his weapon, and said, "By God, they're spies!"

Remarkably, one of the strangers spoke English, and he stepped forward to calm and reassure the townspeople. He told the men nobody was hurt and that everything was all right. He said he would call on "the sheriff" later and fill out a complete report implying that he had some kind of government authority. This is interesting, since few men of Asian descent worked for the U.S.

government in the 1920s due to the racism of the time.

Nonetheless, the strangers were obviously ready to put an end to their meeting with the townsfolk, and the locals could not think of a reason to remain at the crash site. Nobody had been hurt, and apparently no crime had been committed. Finally, the informal posse decided to head back to town, but not before Cole found an interesting item on the ground near the crashed vehicle.

As Cole was looking around, he noticed a strange-looking metallic object on the ground, which he picked up and put in his pocket. He called it a "little thingamajig." He later said, "Here's the funny part. While I was looking around, I spotted a little thingamajig on the ground. I picked it up and decided to keep it. Don't know why I didn't turn it over to one of the foreigners. Anyway, I put it in my pocket." Little did Cole realize at the time that making off with the "thingamajig" would have consequences later.

Exhausted after the evening's events and his long walk out to the crash site and back, Cole went right to bed upon returning to his home in Weston. At 3 in the morning, he was awakened by a furious pounding on his door.

Groggily opening the door, Cole saw a strange-looking individual dressed in what looked like a U.S. Army uniform. Despite the Army uniform, the "man" looked like one of the strangers he had seen earlier standing at the crash site of the object in the forest, having slanted eyes and dark skin.

*Typical U.S. Army Uniform of the 1920s
(YouTube)*

"You picked up something today," the stranger told him. "We need it back."

It took Cole a few minutes to realize what the visitor was wanting from him, finally remembering the metallic "thingamajig" that he had earlier picked up at the crash site. Reaching into the pocket of his coat, Cole retrieved the object and held it out to the stranger, saying, "Is this what you mean?"

Without replying, the visitor snatched the object out of Cole's hand, turned, and walked away into the woods. Cole noticed that he left on foot, obviously having no other means of transportation. Cole shuffled off back to bed.

Cole Found No Evidence in the Grassy Clearing

The next day, Cole grew increasingly puzzled by what transpired in the middle of the night. He began to wonder how the strange individual had managed to find his house and track him down. Cole decided to go back to the site in the forest where the strange object had crashed.

Upon returning to the site, Cole found that the clearing was totally empty. The grass and bushes were all crushed down where the mysterious object had lain, but there was no other evidence of any kind. In the end, was the craft really of alien origin, or could it have been an experimental craft built by the U.S. military in preparation for future wars?

Thinking that perhaps the whole thing was some kind of secret Army project, Cole decided to just forget about the whole thing. He apparently did not mention the incident to anybody until 1967 when he met paranormal researcher John A. Keel while Keel was conducting research on UFO sightings in the area, according to Jerome Clark's book *UFOs from 1960 Through 1979*. Although it is a single witness case that was not disclosed until 43 years after it happened, it remains intriguing, mostly because Keel is considered a careful and thorough researcher.

22

THE SUBMERSIBLE
BOOTLEGGING USO

Hudson River, New York
June 28, 1924

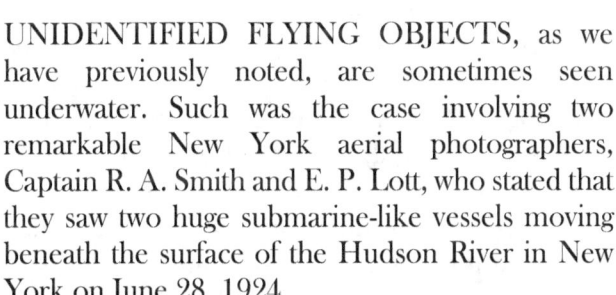

UNIDENTIFIED FLYING OBJECTS, as we have previously noted, are sometimes seen underwater. Such was the case involving two remarkable New York aerial photographers, Captain R. A. Smith and E. P. Lott, who stated that they saw two huge submarine-like vessels moving beneath the surface of the Hudson River in New York on June 28, 1924.

But first, let us discuss the eyewitnesses involved in this case, Smith and Lott. Employed by the Fairchild Aerial Camera Corporation of New York, the two flyers were well-known for their aerial photography, and they later became known for cheating death. Eight months after their UFO sighting, the men crash-landed their plane in the vast wilderness of the Florida Everglades and were believed lost.

Air Posses to Search For Missing New York Flyers

ST. PETERSBURG, Fla., March 29. Rescue parties will be sent in airplanes tomorrow to scour the Everglades for trace of Captain R. A. Smith and E. P. Lott, aerial photographers, believed lost, according to Stuart Moyers, southeastern manager of Fairchild Aerial Surveys for whom the men worked.

Moyers, when notified tonight that the men were thought lost, said he could scarcely believe it, though he had been trying all day to get into communication with Captain Smith over the telephone. He said both were experienced fliers and pilots, and he felt confident they would be able to make a forced landing in safety.

Both Captain Smith and Lott are residents of New York, where they have families. Mrs. Lott flew to Florida with her husband and only returned to New York a few days ago.

Captain Smith served during the war for three years with the British flying forces in France and was later detailed to Canada as an instructor in aerial photography. Mr. Lott was a member of the American flying forces during the war.

Mr. Moyers said a Curtiss plane would be secured from some local aviator and the search would be begun as early as possible in the morning, in the event no word is received of the men up to that time. At the same time an order will go to headquarters to send a machine with a pilot to continue the search until the men are found.

The Miami (Florida) Herald, March 30, 1925, p. 1

The *Miami Herald* declared, "Rescue parties will be sent in airplanes tomorrow to scour the Everglades for trace of Captain R. A. Smith and E. P. Lott, aerial photographers, believed lost...."

Three days after their plane went down, the aviators were spotted by search planes that were combing the area, fearing the worst. Smith and Lott were alive and well, having put down their plane "beside a little creek" after a cracked cylinder in their engine forced the emergency landing. When they were found, the men were in the process of repairing the engine and were "little the worse for their experience."

On June 28, 1924, Lott and Smith were in a small plane, engaged in photography over the Hudson River near the city of Ossining, New York, when they saw something very strange moving below the surface of the river.

Flying at about 5,500 feet above the river, the aviators saw two "immense objects" moving upstream and somewhat below the surface of the water. The objects were about 250 feet in length and were moving parallel to each other, about 600 feet apart.

With his aerial survey camera, equipped with a telephoto lens, Smith took a photograph, which shows two cylindrical objects that came to a point at their bow. Behind each strange craft was a disturbed flow of water (called a Kelvin wake) shaped like an arrow, which some people thought could have been caused by a periscope protruding above the surface of the water.

Simulation of Kelvin Wake

(By L3erdnik - Own work, CC BY-SA 4.0,

https://commons.wikimedia.org/w/index.php?curid=71068896)

Dry Agents Seek Submarine Rum Runner in Hudson River

NEW YORK, June 28.—Prohibition officials began a search for rum-running U-boats in the Hudson river.

Their unusual quest was inspired by the report of aerial photographers who turned over to them a picture snapped 5,500 feet above the waters of the Hudson showing two queer looking craft proceeding up the river opposite Sing Sing prison at Ossining.

D. P. Lott, pilot of the photographers' plane and R. A. Smith, an advertising photographer, made the discovery. Casually looking downward as the plane flew up the river

Smith said the two objects attracted his attention and he made a picture with the use of a telephoto lens.

The picture shows dimly two long objects apparently about 250 feet in length, driving upstream under the surface of the water and about 600 feet apart. The photograph shows a wash of water similar to the wake left by a periscope. It was this circumstance that led the prohibition officials to believe that rum-runners may now be resorting to submarine boats to smuggle liquor into New York.

Navy department officials said that no submarines were known to be in these waters at this time.

The Buffalo (N.Y.) Times, June 28, 1924, p. 11

Unfortunately, the photograph taken by Smith has not been located in the historical archives and may be lost forever. However, we do have accounts from persons who saw the photo and were able to describe it.

A theory was advanced that Lott and Smith saw a "rum runner" using a submarine to illegally smuggle alcohol. This possibility caused government agents to begin combing the Hudson River looking for the clandestine underwater craft. Since smugglers often did use boats on the Hudson for their illicit activities, the use of submarines may sound plausible; however, history tells us that there were no instances of submarines being employed by smugglers at any point in the 1920s. Clearly, the theory did not pan out.

It was also speculated that Lott and Smith may have seen a U. S. Navy submarine, but this explanation seems unlikely due to the size of the objects that the aviators observed. The Navy's primary submarines of the time were the O-class vessels developed for World War I and used during World War II. They were typically about 172 feet in length and 18 feet at their widest points. The Navy denied having any submarine operations underway in the Hudson River during the time period of the strange sighting.

Photo # NH 99962   USS O-1 underway

U.S. Navy O-Class Submarine, Circa 1917

In the end, this sighting remains unexplained to this day. It has been referenced in a number of publications about paranormal phenomena, including Jerome Clark's 2013 book *Unexplained: Strange Sightings, Incredible Occurrences, and Puzzling Physical Phenomena.*

IS MARS INHABITED?
1924 MAY REVEAL IT

Star Sleuths Prepare to Solve
Mystery When Planet Whirls to
Within 35,000,000 Miles.

MANY THEORIES ADVANCED

Scientific Eyes to Strain at Telescopes and Wireless to Be Tried to Read Sky Secret.

New York Times, Sept. 18, 1921, p. 25

23

CLEAR THE AIRWAVES FOR MARS

Washington, D. C.
August 21-24, 1924

BELIEVING THAT INTELLIGENT life might exist on Mars and that it might be trying to contact humanity, a number of government officials and scientists in 1924 came up with a plan to silence all radio communications during the three days that the two planets were closest in proximity to each other.

Whereas Mars at times can be as far as 250 million miles from Earth, in August 1924, it approached to within 36 million miles. As a result, the initiative was launched to try to hear whatever messages Mars might be sending to us.

The Brooklyn (N.Y) Daily Eagle,
Aug. 24, 1914, p. 63

Among those who believed that communication might be possible was Curtis D. Wilbur, Secretary of the U.S. Navy. From Washington, D. C., Wilbur's department sent orders to every naval station throughout the nation, stating, "The Navy desires to cooperate with astronomers who believe it possible that Mars may attempt communication by radio waves with this planet while they are near together. All shore radio stations will especially note and report any electrical phenomenon of an unusual character."

Naval radio operators were asked to keep the lines open and manned between August 21 and August 24, ready to receive any Martian missives.

For a number of years prior to 1924, interest had grown in trying to communicate with Mars. As far back as 1894, Sir William Henry Preece, a British engineer and radio enthusiast, proposed signaling the far planet. Seven years later, American scientist and inventor Nikolas Tesla announced that he believed he had intercepted messages from either Mars or Venus. Also, more recently, in 1921, Italian scientist Guglielmo Marconi suggested that he too had received strange signals from Mars.

Thus it was that the idea of establishing contact with Mars grew exponentially as the time of Earth's closest approach to Mars grew nearer.

'MYSTERY' MESSAGE REPEATED TODAY STIRS RADIO MEN

Unearthly 'Z-Z-Z-Zipps' in Ordered Sequence Are Possibly of Martian Origin—and Possibly Not

By United Press Leased Wire.

VANCOUVER, B. C., Aug. 22.—"Mystery signals" heard on the radio at Point Grey, near Vancouver, last night, by operators listening for a message from Mars," were again heard at 7:14 a.m. today.

Operators at the Point Grey radio station and W. G. Walker, radio expert, and connected with the Vancouver Merchants Exchange listening independently, heard the signals.

The Pomona (Calif.) Progress Bulletin,
Aug. 22, 1924, p. 1

Finally, the highly anticipated event came to pass. Radio receivers in both the United States and Europe were cleared of all traffic, and all ears were prepared to receive the first momentous message from the planet Mars.

QUEER SIGNALS HEARD.

Norfolk Men Think They May Have Come From Mars.

NORFOLK, Va., August 23.—Queer radio signals were picked up here yesterday. As to whether they had any connection with the visit of the planet Mars or were merely a coincidence, local wireless experts would not venture an opinion.

Just before 1 o'clock and shortly after Government sending stations had broadcast orders to all naval receiving stations to be on the alert for any possible Martian messages, B. A. Mabry and B. G. Cowan, in charge of the powerful receiving set in the office of the chief dispatcher of the Atlantic Coast Line Railway, picked up a message unlike anything they had ever heard.

The message was not in any known code and the tone was declared as "distant and warbling, like a faraway train whistle." As near as they could make out, the radio men said, the signals corresponded to WF in the Universal code, but was composed of a queer mixture of dots and dashes. It continued for about 15 minutes.

The railway set, one of the most powerful in this section, was tuned in at 2,300 meters. Both Mabry and Cowan are veteran operators.

Evening Star (Washington, D.C.),
Aug. 23, 1924, p. 1

On the first evening of the radio silence "window," August 21, mystery signals were picked up in Vancouver, British Columbia. The sounds were described as "unearthly z-z-z-zipps."

The following day, "queer" signals were picked up at a radio station in Norfolk, Virginia. A newspaper reporter wrote, "The message was not in any known code and the tone was declared as distant and warbling, like a faraway train whistle." The strange sounds, received in the 2,300-meter range, continued for about 15 minutes.

Americans were incredibly interested in the idea of hearing signals from Mars, and many people showed up at astronomical observatories throughout the nation. More than 300 visitors crowded the observatory at Drake University in Iowa.

In the end, except for a few mysterious noises that might have been caused by any number of sources on Earth, not much else was heard during the three days of radio silence.

According to *AtlasObscura.com*: "The opposition came and went with no extraterrestrial message. As far as anyone can tell, the Navy's few days of silence yielded nothing but static. It was the same for the British scientists. But that hasn't stopped us from trying to communicate with anyone who's listening. And even when our planets are at their closest in the celestial dance, it's all relative. The space between us is still vast, and any Earthlings looking up at that orange spot might still feel alone."

Ford Model T
ModelTMitch, CC BY-SA 4.0 via Wikimedia Commons

24

300-FOOT-LONG UFO

Near Chicago, Illinois
June 1925

ON A LONELY ROAD just north of Chicago, Illinois, in June 1925, a motorist driving his Ford Model T car at 2:30 a.m. saw a jaw-dropping sight flying in the night sky above him. Also in the car with him was at least one passenger. The incident was reported in the *San Diego (Calif.) Evening Tribune*, on August 12, 1965.

The witnesses, whose identities were not given, saw a huge cigar-shaped UFO, which they estimated to be about 300 feet in length. Along the sides of the ship were rows of multicolored lights "It was a lot of colors, such as blue, red, white, green," the driver said.

Bringing his Model T to a stop in order to have a better look, the driver noticed that the object was emitting sparks from its front end. "Red sparks were flying away from its nose."

Also, along the side of the object, he noticed illuminated windows. "About 100 feet down through the center [was] all lit up with windows."

Cylindrical UFO by Artist Neil Riebe

Another important aspect to the sighting was a sensation of intense heat felt by the witnesses, coming from the UFO as it neared their position. "As it passed in front of us, a heat wave came down from it," the driver said.

Though the encounter was a brief one, it is certainly notable in the annals of ufology.

25

THE UFOS
THAT LIVED

Battle Mountain, Nevada
1925

IN 1959, UFO RESEARCHER and publisher Raymond A. Palmer (1910-1977) received a letter from an eyewitness to a bizarre event that happened in 1925 on Flat Mesa, near Battle Mountain, Nevada. On the surface, the story appears to be a UFO sighting, except that the objects he saw apparently were living creatures.

Palmer, co-founder of *Fate* magazine and one-time editor of *Amazing Stories*, was a leading figure in ufology in the 1940s and 1950s. In the very first issue of *Fate*, he published the story of pilot Kenneth Arnold's UFO sighting that is considered to mark the beginning of the modern UFO era.

UFOs IN THE ROARING TWENTIES

The explosion of UFO sightings in the 1950s led Palmer to create *Flying Saucers* magazine, which existed from 1957 to 1976. The story about "living" UFOs in the Nevada Desert is among the most unusual that he ran in the magazine.

World War I era "Jenny" Monoplane (Wikipedia)

Palmer received the letter from a gentleman named Don Wood, Jr., who related his amazing experience from 1925. Wood stated that he and three other aviators were flying World War I era monoplanes over the Nevada desert. "We landed on Flat Mesa, near Battle Mountain, Nevada. The mesa is about five thousand square feet and the walls are too steep to climb unless a lot of work is done."

Wood continued, "We wanted to see what was on top of this flat place. We landed at one o'clock in the afternoon. While walking about the top of this place, we noticed something coming in for a landing. It was about eight feet across and was round and flat like a saucer. The undersides were a reddish color."

According to Wood, the object skidded to a stop a short distance away, and the curious humans approached it to further examine it. "We walked up to the thing and it was some animal like we never saw before. It was hurt, and as it breathed, the top would rise and fall, making a half-foot hole all around it like a clam opening and closing."

"Quite a hunk had been chewed out of one side of this rim and a sort of metal-looking froth issued. When it saw us, it breathed frantically and rose up only a few inches, only to fall back to the earth again. It was moist and glistened on the top side. We could see no eyes or legs." He added that it had a "micalike shell body."

After about twenty minutes, a similar creature, except larger, came in for a landing close beside the first. "Four sucker-like tongues settled on the little one, and the big one got so dazzlingly bright, you couldn't look at it. Both rose straight up and were out of sight in a second. They must have been traveling a thousand miles an hour to get so high so fast."

After the creatures departed, Wood and his companions found "frothy" metallic debris that looked like "fine aluminum wire" where the creatures had been. The strange material soon melted in the blazing desert sun.

This amazing story has been featured in a number of publications about UFOs and about unexplained beasts (cryptoids) over the years, including in the book *Other Worlds, Other*

Universes by Brad Steiger and John White, published in 1975. Some researchers believe that the creatures seen on Flat Mesa in 1925 were a strange form of life that lives in the Earth's atmosphere and rarely descends to our planet's surface.

A Typical Nevada Mesa (Needpix.com)

According to *Crypid Wiki*, "Atmospheric beasts are the strangest of the flying monsters from ufology, cryptozoology and astrobiology. According to eyewitness reports, they are things that seem like living creatures, but they break all the usual rules that we apply to living things. They fly without the need for wings and their bodies are only semi-solid, often partially invisible."

Some researchers feel that this story would be more believable if it had been reported closer in time to when it actually happened, instead of 34 years later. When it was finally reported, in 1959, UFOs had become a very popular topic in North America. Also, many science-fiction films and TV shows had become part of popular culture, featuring flying saucers, aliens, and other strange paranormal creatures.

So, a dose of skepticism is always a good thing, especially in analyzing cases like this one. While Wood and his friends may well have seen an atmospheric beast similar to the famous "Crawfordsville Monster" of 1891, perhaps it resulted from an overactive imagination fueled by the flying saucer mania of the late 1950s.

Brown Mountain (2013 Photo by Jan Kronsell)
CC BY-SA (https://creativecommons.org/licenses/by-sa/4.0)

26

STRANGE LIGHTS
ON BROWN
MOUNTAIN

Brown Mountain, North Carolina
November 7, 1925

ON NOVEMBER 7, 1925, the magazine *Literary Digest* published an account of sightings of mysterious lights in and around Brown Mountain, North Carolina. Although the lights had been seen for a number of years prior, the article titled "The Queer Lights on Brown Mountain" established these strange lights as a true unexplained phenomenon.

The article said, "Brown Mountain, Burke County, North Carolina, has some very spooky lights.... Some of the native citizens say the lights are as old as the Civil War; others have known them for a quarter of a century.... Some people who have been observing these strange lights for many years say they are of supernatural origin ...."

Weighing in on the mysterious lights, paranormal researcher Charles Fort said, in his book *Lo!*, "From time to time, luminous objects, or beings, have been reported from Brown Mountain, North Carolina...... The luminosities travel, as if with motions of their own. They are brilliant, globular forms, and move in the sky, with a leisureliness and duration that exclude any explanation in meteoric terms."

> From time to time, luminous objects, or beings, have been reported from Brown Mountain, North Carolina. They appear, and then for a long time are not seen, and then they appear again. See the *Literary Digest*, Nov. 7, 1925. I have other records. The luminosities travel, as if with motions of their own. They are brilliant, globular forms, and move in the sky, with a leisureliness and duration that exclude any explanation in meteoric terms.

Lo! by Charles Fort, p. 84

Robert Sparks Walker, an eyewitness to the phenomenon, wrote the following description in 1925: "What would you think or say, if you were standing on Rattlesnake Knob, on the Morganton, North Carolina, road about 7:30 p.m. and saw in a southeasterly direction a curious light, about the size of a toy balloon, smaller than the full moon, and very red, rise mysteriously over Brown Mountain, proceed into the air a short distance, waver as if it were palsied, and then in less than a minute disappear?"

Photo by Steve Baxter from Pexels.com

Walker continued, "The descriptions of the strange light made by various observers do not agree. One person says it is pale white, ordinarily observed through a ground-glass globe, with a faint, irregular halo encircling it. He claims that it is restricted to a prescribed circle and appears from three to four times in rapid succession, then conceals itself for twenty minutes, when it reappears within the same circle. Another observer, who was standing about eight miles from Brown Mountain, says that suddenly after sunset there blazed into the sky above the mountain a steady glowing ball of light. To him, the light appeared yellowish, and it lasted about half a minute, when it disappeared rather abruptly. It appeared to him like a star from a bursting skyrocket, but much brighter."

On other occasions, the strange lights were seen going up into the sky from the mountaintop and moving rapidly away far into the sky until they were out of sight.

A very early description of the phenomenon appears in the September 24, 1913 edition of the

Charlotte Daily Observer, in which a fisherman claimed to have seen "mysterious lights ... just above the horizon every night, red in color, with a pronounced circular shape." Another account, in the September 26, 1913 edition of *The Lenoir (N.C.) Topic,* said, "According to a news item from Linville Falls, the folks of that section are 'seein' things.' The mysterious light that is seen just above the horizon almost every night from Rattlesnake Knob, near Cold Spring, on the Morganton road, about 7 miles from here, is baffling all investigators. All theories as to its nature or origin have either been exploded or fell through from lack of evidence to support them.

"With punctual regularity, the light rises in a southeasterly direction from the point of observation, just over the slope of Brown Mountain, first about 7:30 p.m., again about 20 minutes later and again at 10 o'clock. It looks much like a toy tire balloon, a distinct ball, with no atmosphere about it. It rises in the far distance or about six miles from Rattlesnake Knob, and after going up a short distance, wavers and goes out in less than a minute."

The Brown Mountain Lights are still with us today and have been featured in publications, television shows, movies, and on web sites. They were mentioned in the 1999 episode "Field Trip" of the paranormal TV series *The X Files,* as well as in episodes of *Ancient Aliens, Mystery Hunters,* and *Weird or What?*

27
FAMOUS PILOT ENCOUNTERS UFOS

Near Wichita Kansas
January 1926

ONE OF AMERICA'S greatest early airplane pilots was San Diego, California, native Bertrand "Bert" Acosta (1895-1954), who taught himself to fly at age 15 and later became a flight instructor for both the U.S. and Canadian militaries. During his aviation career, Acosta set a number of airspeed records and achieved fame in other ways. What many people do not realize is that Acosta was one of the very first pilots to report having encountered several UFOs while flying.

In testimony collected by Richard Hall of the National Investigations Committee on Aerial Phenomena (NICAP), Acosta's amazing UFO encounter is disclosed.

Photos of Bert Acosta from The Akron Beacon Journal (Akron, Ohio), Feb. 12, 1939, p. 53

On a day in January of 1926, at 1 p.m., Acosta was flying by himself from Wichita, Kansas to Colorado Springs, Colorado, when he saw six, shiny disc-shaped objects flying about 200 yards off his right wing. The discs, which were of "unconventional appearance and aerobatic performance," then approached closer and began circling his plane. Describing the objects as "flying manhole covers," Acosta said each disc was between three and five feet in diameter.

Circling around his airplane, these strange craft approached to within ten feet of Acosta's plane. They exhibited "a discontinuous trajectory. i.e., vertical drops, maneuvers or loops," according to renowned UFO researcher Jacques Vallée. The maneuvers continued for between two and five minutes, before the shiny discs suddenly changed course and rapidly flew away.

This sighting was first disclosed in the 1960s by two of the major UFO researchers of that era, Vallée and Richard Hall. The case has been mentioned in a number of publications over the years, including the book *Unidentified Aerial Phenomena - Eighty Years of Pilot Sightings* by Dominique Weinstein, published in 2001 by the National Aviation Reporting Center on Anomalous Phenomena (NARCAP).

Bert Acosta (right) from Philadelphia Inquirer, Apr. 15, 1927, p. 1

Of greatest significance in this case is that the principal eyewitness was one of America's most decorated early pilots. We have been unable to find any accounts of the incident from the time period in which it happened, since it is clear that Acosta did not report the encounter until later in his life, at some point prior to his death from tuberculosis at age 59 in 1954.

Upon his death, one obituary proclaimed, "During his fabulous lifetime, Acosta was in turn a World War I flight instructor, pathfinder for the U.S. air mail service, holder of the 1921 world speed record, and coholder of a flight endurance mark."

> The first pilot observation is an old one dating back to the early 1920's, and is similar to the cases reported today. According to UFO researchers Frank Edwards and Jacques Vallee, pilot Bert Acosta was flying in the Southwestern U.S. when he was stunned to see a half dozen circular objects flying 200 yards off his right wing. He described them as l o o king similar to "manhole covers." They followed in position for 5 minutes, then changed course and flew away. Acosta had no idea what they were, but was positive they were real.

New Castle (Pennsylvania) News,
Nov. 5, 1966, p. 13

28

FIRST STEP
INTO SPACE

Auburn, Massachusetts
March 16, 1926

BY THE 1920s, humanity was fully invested in the idea of manned flight. It had started with hot air balloons before progressing to dirigibles and then airplanes. The next step in the evolution was spacecraft, conceptually analogous to the mysterious UFOs that had been seen throughout the planet for centuries prior. Even in the 1920s, technology that would hurl men into outer space was much closer to becoming a reality than many people thought.

For the most part, the "Space Age" began on March 16, 1926 when Robert H. Goddard launched the world's first liquid-fueled rocket in Auburn, Massachusetts. The rocket rose just 41 feet during a two-and-a-half second flight that ended 184 feet away in a cabbage field, but it was an important demonstration that liquid fuels and oxidizers were possible propellants for larger rockets. It represented mankind's first step into outer space. Using these core principles of rocketry, humanity landed upon the surface of the moon a mere 42 years after Goddard's first rocket launch.

> **Moon Rocket**
>
> **Q.** Has anyone succeeded in sending a rocket to the moon?
>
> **A.** Professor Robert H. Goddard, of Clark University, Worcester, Mass. for a number of years has been working on the idea of a rocket which can be propelled outside of the predominating gravitational field of the earth which might reach the moon. His present effort, however, is merely to construct a small rocket to explore the upper atmosphere of the earth.

The Oklahoma News, 12-4-1926, p. 4

As early as 1921, Goddard had stated that it was his intention to create a self-propelled rocket capable of reaching the moon. He told newspapers at the time that "preliminary experiments and theoretical calculations" had convinced him that it was possible to build "a self-propelling rocket capable of overcoming the earth's attraction, successive explosions of nitro-cellulose maintaining an average speed of two miles a second, which would take it to the moon in 36 hours."

Robert Goddard - March 16, 1926

Before a rocket to the moon could happen, Goddard would have to focus on the basics of perfecting his rocket launch system. Although not too many people in the United States seemed to be taking Goddard's experiments very seriously, scientists elsewhere in the world were very interested – one of them being a German scientist named Hermann Oberth, who exchanged letters with Goddard and sought ways to expand on Goddard's theories.

By 1926, Oberth was convinced that by applying and amplifying Goddard's theories, he could construct a rocket large enough to transport two persons to the moon. In addition to Oberth, scientists in Russia were also closely studying Goddard's work in America.

Dr. Robert Hutchings Goddard (left) and Hermann Oberth (right)

Amazingly, although the world's first airplane flight had occurred only 23 years earlier, the idea of developing a method to reach the moon was already well underway among leading scientists.

As we have seen, Goddard's experiments heavily influenced Oberth, who in turn influenced Wernher von Braun, his 18-year-old lab assistant in Germany. Drawing on the expertise of Goddard, and the refinements to Goddard's work made by Oberth, von Braun proceeded to develop Nazi Germany's rocket program and the notorious V-2 rocket. After World War II ended, von Braun was taken captive by the United States, and he used his rocket expertise, gleaned from Goddard and Oberth, to build America's space program and the rocket technology that landed humankind upon the moon in 1969. The humble technology that Goddard had demonstrated by launching the world's first liquid-fueled rocket in 1926 had finally resulted in what he had hoped – a trip to the moon.

In an interesting footnote upon which to end this chapter, Oberth was a strong believer that UFOs exist and that they are extraterrestrial in nature. In 1954, he told *The American Weekly* magazine, "It is my thesis that flying saucers are real, and that they are spaceships from another solar system. I think that they possibly are manned by intelligent observers who are members of a race that may have been investigating our earth for centuries...."

He later added, "Having weighed all the pros and cons, I find the explanation of flying discs from outer space the most likely one."

It is utterly fascinating that the man who, along with Robert Goddard, was instrumental in helping human beings travel into space was inspired, at least in part, by his belief that Earth had, for long ages, been visited by beings from other solar systems using spaceships of an extremely advanced design. Is it any wonder that he was motivated to develop a means, given the crude technologies available in the twentieth century, to travel into the realm from which these mysterious beings came?

29

FLEET OF UFOS

Westmont, Illinois
August 1926

8-YEAR-OLD Frank John Tezky and his father, Joseph Tezky, observed a fleet of UFOs passing overhead in their hometown of Westmont, Illinois, in August 1926.

They first saw a large disc-shaped object moving west beneath cirrus clouds. Then they saw five smaller discs trailing in a straight line behind the larger one.

The Tezkys noticed that the nearby clouds were reflecting the light that was emanating from the six discs.

What is unusual about this sighting is the presence of a large UFO, possibly a mothership, trailed by significantly smaller craft. In other UFO cases involving motherships, often smaller craft are seen coming out of the larger one. By definition, a mothership serves as a platform from which smaller ships are launched. *Wikipedia* gives this definition: "... a large vehicle that leads, serves, or carries other smaller vehicles. A mother ship may be a maritime ship, aircraft, or spacecraft."

Image by ELG21 from Pixabay

Also interesting about this case is that the UFOs were highly illuminated, such that the light from them shone on nearby clouds. Although it is unclear whether this was a daylight or nighttime sighting, the intensity of the illumination is interesting, indeed.

Historical documents verify that Frank John Tezky was born in 1918 in Chicago, Illinois, and entered military service in 1941. He later became a lieutenant colonel in the U.S. Air Force. He also obtained a master's degree in education. Tezky passed away on April 20, 2014, at the age of 96.

His sighting was mentioned in the article "UFOs of the Roaring '20s," by Jerome Clark and Lucius Farish, appearing in the Fall 1975 edition of *Saga UFO Report*. It was also referenced in Jerome Clark's *UFO Encyclopedia.*

30

AIRPLANE
ENCOUNTERS UFO

Near Salt Lake City, Utah
September 1926

As reported by the National Aviation Reporting Center on Anomalous Phenomena (NARCAP) in a book titled *Unidentified Aerial Phenomena – Eighty Years of Pilot Sightings* (Dominique Weinstein, Feb. 2001), a U.S. air mail airplane encountered a "cylindrical huge object, wingless," which caused the pilot to make an emergency landing from the skies over Nevada in September of 1926. The incident was also reported by Richard Hall of the National Investigations Committee on Aerial Phenomena (NICAP) in his 1964 book *The UFO Evidence.*

The air mail pilot, flying a DeHavilland DH-4 Biplane, stated that the encounter happened at 11 p.m., while he was en route to Salt Lake City, Utah. According to the report filed with NICAP, the airplane pilot witnessed a long, cylindrical object that subsequently approached to within 50 yards of the DH-4.

1923 Postage Stamp Showing a DH-4 Air Mail Plane

Upon nearing the strange object, the airplane's engine began to sputter and misfire, forcing the pilot to make an emergency landing on a pasture down below.

After the encounter, the cigar-shaped object "took off like a shot out of a gun," speeding away rapidly.

The NICAP report states the following:

September 1926; Nr. Salt Lake City, UT
11:00 PM. An air mail pilot was repeatedly buzzed by a long, cylindrical object. Each time the object came within about 50 yards, the aircraft engine would begin to sputter and misfire, until the pilot was forced to make an emergency landing in a pasture. At this point the UFO "took off like a shot out of a gun" and sped away. (Hall, 2000, p. 13).

Restored 1926 DH-4 at the Historic Aircraft Restoration Museum in St. Louis, Missouri (By Tim Vickers Public Domain)

What is incredibly intriguing about this sighting is that it is one of the earliest encounters between an aircraft and a UFO. In addition, the shape of the UFO (large, wingless, and cylindrical) is very unique for the time period in which it was reported. Blimp-like shapes with "wings" and rudder-like devices were, of course, seen often in the late 1800s and early 1900s. But perhaps the most amazing detail in this case is the report that proximity to the object caused the aircraft's engine to "sputter and misfire."

Typical Cylindrical UFO (1967 Photo)

This airborne UFO encounter was vetted by a number of UFO researchers that are well-known for their high standards and careful approach, including Richard Hall of NICAP, who was later involved with a number of other UFO research organizations, including the Mutual UFO Network (MUFON) and the Fund for UFO Research (FUFOR). Hall, called "the dean of ufology," was known as a strong believer in the theory that UFOs are extraterrestrial spacecraft from an advanced alien civilization.

Although the primary source of this 1926 encounter is not known, it is likely that the pilot involved in the case contacted either NARCAP or NICAP at some point in the 1950s or 1960s. It also seems probable that his eyewitness testimony was taken down by Richard Hall and then, after a measure of research and verification, the case was published in the 1964 book *The UFO Evidence*, which was a compilation of cases from the NICAP archives.

DH-4B Biplane (Public Domain)

31

THE UFO IN THE PHOTOGRAPH

Cave Junction, Oregon
1927

ALTHOUGH IT IS NOT without controversy, a photograph purportedly taken in 1927 is considered one of the best of America's early UFO pictures. The monochromatic photo very clearly shows a saucer shaped flying object with a flattened dome on top in the sky among the clouds. Technically, it is a "domed disc" and the sighting is considered a "daylight disc."

The location of the photo is Cave Junction, Oregon, a town established in 1926 and originally known as Cave City. The town served as the gateway to the newly founded Oregon Caves Monument, which was established in 1909 by President William Howard Taft under the auspices of the U.S. Forest Service.

The date of the photo is believed to be either 1926 or 1927. Since the town was founded in 1926 and was being developed during this time, it was a period of busy activity such as construction of buildings, roads, and railroads. A lot of people were outside during the daytime, which could have easily led to the sighting of UFOs such as in the photograph under discussion.

Close-up of UFO in Cave Junction Photograph

The photographer's name is unknown. He is believed to have been a volunteer fireman in the area of Cave City, Oregon.

2. DOMED DISC				

Dome-Shaped UFO from NICAP Chart (1964)

What is most impressive about his photo is that, during the time in which it was taken, the tools for creating a photographic "fake" were extremely limited. In his book *UFOs Caught on Film: Amazing Evidence of Alien Visitors to Earth* by B. J. Booth, the author says, "In the late twenties, when this was taken, it was quite hard to fake a photograph ... Anyone seeing the photograph at the time would have called it a 'spaceship.'"

Cave Junction Area in 2013 (Photo by Dicie Hinaga)

In his 2018 book *UFO Photos: Computer Analysis of Worldwide UFO Images Through the Decades,* Jason Gleaves said this photo "is certainly interesting" and that "it is an early quality image which has been in ufology circulation way before the term 'flying saucer' had ever been spoken. The clear crisp image for its age was reportedly taken by a volunteer fire fighter who resided in the local Oregon area. The image has a slight yellowing/fading configuration overall, which is consistent with photographs of that era and natural age deterioration."

In the end, this is one of best UFO photographs from the early part of the 20th century, and it directly flies in the face of the argument that no "flying saucer" shapes had been seen anywhere in the world until the 1940s. The image captured in this photo is clearly a classic UFO disc, similar to what has been photographed many times since 1947.

Oregon Caves National Monument in 2018

(Photo by daveynin via Flickr)

https://creativecommons.org/licenses/by/2.0/

32

FAMOUS POET
SEES UFO

Sausalito, California
February 1927

IRISH-BORN POET Ella Young (1867-1956),
who immigrated to the United States in 1925 and
lived in Sausalito, California, during the mid-1920s,
had a remarkable UFO sighting in February 1927
while sitting outside the Casa Madrid Hotel & Spa
in Sausalito. An expert in Celtic mythology who
often gave lectures while dressed in purple Druid
robes, Young told of her sighting in a letter to
Meade Layne (1882-1961), an early UFO
researcher.

Irish Poet Visiting In L. A. This Week

ELLA YOUNG

Ella Young, noted Irish poet and story teller, is to be in Los Angeles through the courtesy of the Los Angeles Public Library and the Los Angeles Booksellers' Association for appearances during Children's Book Week (November 17 to 24). She will also be the guest of various stores and clubs in Southern California.

The Ventura County Star and the
Ventura Daily Post
(Ventura, California)
Nov. 18, 1929, p. 5

Young's letter was later published in the book *Flying Saucers on the Attack* by Harold T. Wilkins, in which she described her sighting as follows: "I believe I saw a space ship early in 1927, at the Casa Madrona Hotel, Sausalito (Marin County, California). I was, one morning, sitting outside the hotel, thinking of nothing in particular, when I saw a cigar-shaped craft shoot out of a cloud beyond the bay, and across the sky towards Tamalpais. At first, I thought it must be a U.S. airship, but soon changed my mind. It was not shaped like the *Akron* [a famous dirigible of the time]. It was long and slender, of yellow colour, and travelling at great speed. As it came opposite me, it seemed to progress by alternately contracting and elongating its body."

The sighting occurred at approximately 9 a.m.

Interestingly, Ella Young was a believer in the literal existence of fairies and dwarves (i.e. little people). Some researchers have noted that many similarities exist between UFO beings and fairies. Some have even said that aliens are the modern-day equivalent of ancient stories about fairies and dwarves.

Meade Layne

During an interview with immigration agents, Young spoke about her belief in fairies, and her comment temporarily delayed her request to emigrate to the U.S. because she was suspected of being "mentally unstable." She was, however, later approved.

The recipient of her letter about her UFO sighting, Meade Layne, was a believer in the theory that UFOs come from a parallel dimension, rather than from outer space. He called the other dimension "Etheria" and claimed that the world's governments were aware of Etheria's existence.

33

REVOLVING UFO

West Frankfort, Illinois
1927

AN EYEWITNESS IDENTIFIED only as "Mr. Jones" saw an amazing, large UFO hovering over a house in his neighborhood, in West Frankford, Illinois, in 1927. His description of the object is fascinating.

The object was a large round sphere, about 40 feet in diameter. Its width was roughly the same as the width of the house over which it was hovering. Its hull seemed to be like stainless steel and was completely smooth, unmarked by seams or rivets.

When Jones first saw it, the UFO was in motion and was revolving from right to left. Then it came to a stop, and the revolving motion stopped.

Airship with Gondola (FreeSVG.com)

Underneath the spherical part of the UFO was attached a "gondola," on the surface of which there suddenly appeared four or five illuminated "portholes." The light shining through from inside the gondola was a bluish-white.

As Jones watched the bizarre object, he noticed that it drifted to the right about 100 feet before stopping again. Then, out of its bottom section, came a thin, reflecting pipe or rod, extending downward. Jones thought it might have been a rod made of glass or perhaps a very thin piece of pipe or wire.

Eventually, the illuminated portholes closed, which the witness said looked like the closing of the "iris shutter" of a camera. After the portholes closed, the UFO began rotating again, and then it zoomed away in the same direction whence it had come.

The sighting was reported in an article called "UFOs of the Roaring 20s," by Jerome Clark and Lucius Farish, published in *UFO Report*, February 1980.

Camden, New Jersey, Circa 1927

34
CAMDEN'S COSMIC SNIPER

Camden, New Jersey
1927 - 1928

FROM NOVEMBER OF 1927 through late February of 1928, Camden, New Jersey, was plagued by what the press dubbed a "phantom sniper." It was so christened because it was as though an unseen sniper was raining down invisible bullets on his victims.

Windshields of vehicles driving along the Camden Bridge would suddenly find themselves pierced by unseen projectiles. What made the event fall into the paranormal realm wasn't the fact that the shooter couldn't be found, it was because no bullets could be found embedded in the vehicles. Only the entry points through the glass, when it didn't shatter completely, could be found. This was no case of "Yellow Journalism" (a.k.a. Fake News), either, as there were numerous articles on the subject with photographs of the victims and witnesses.

It all began on November 21, 1927, with a former state senator, Albert S. Woodruff, who was fired upon in his automobile while he was driving across the Federal Street Bridge. Woodruff claimed to hear a noise akin to a gunshot, when suddenly a projectile came through his windshield. However, no bullet was ever found. Oddly, Woodruff was one of the only victims of the sniper to ever hear a gunshot. Typically, there was no sound of a gunshot.

More people were fired upon in the area after this, and the street lights along the Camden Bridge were shot out as well. Mrs. A. D. Kohn was driving along the bridge when her vehicle was struck by the invisible bullets. She was injured by the shattered glass, but not the bullet, which again could not be found.

Though police were certainly puzzled by the reports that came in off and on throughout the month of December, the phantom sniper didn't become a media sensation until an article published in the *Camden Courier-Post* on January 25, 1928, reported how the "ghost sniper" had fired upon a bus and a police officer. It began by stating, "Probing a mystery that sounds more like fantastic fiction than serious fact, police of Camden and officials of the Camden Bridge today were conducting a vigorous hunt for a 'phantom sniper.'"

The article reported that a lone bullet had penetrated the windshield of a Pennsylvania bus on the Camden Bridge. According to witness testimony, before this happened, the driver, Franklin Copeland, said he heard "a sudden buzz." A passenger by the name of Harriet Billingsley said she saw a brief flash of light, but she was the only one of the seven passengers that did. The article stated that after Copeland heard the buzzing noise that "as if by magic a small hole appeared in the glass before his face."

Copeland slammed on the brakes as passengers were "half thrown from their seats and cried out to know what was wrong." A witness on the streets identified as Clarke came running to the bus. He noticed the bullet hole in the glass and began to look around for possible shooters, but all he saw was a "little girl who strolled on."

After the shooting, Bridge Policeman John J. Rodgers was sent out to investigate. At 4:30 A.M. he was struck between the shoulders and knocked down.

Whatever hit Rodgers, it didn't penetrate his skin. Moments later he found a blue marble rolling on the ground, and assumed that's what hit him. Initially we assumed that the blue marble was purely circumstantial evidence, as typically no projectiles were ever found again in future cases. For instance, perhaps the blue marble was already laying on the bridge, misplaced by the little girl seen earlier? When Rodgers found it, it seemed to him to be the only logical explanation. However, the pesky blue marble would make a repeat appearance later.

Photo Published in the January 25ᵗʰ Article Showing where the Bus was Shot (1) and where Rogers (pictured in inset) was shot (2).

The newspaper article states, "Police were unanimous in the opinion that the missile which penetrated the window of the bus on the span yesterday was no such marble, but a bullet." However, just to reiterate once more, no "bullet" was found embedded in the bus anywhere.

Because no gunshot was heard, police considered the theory that a slingshot or air gun was the tool of the phantom sniper, "but other officers insisted that no instrument of this nature would discharge a bullet, ball bearing or other metal missile with sufficient force to bore through the windshields of buses and automobiles," the paper reported.

Gottlob Meyer (inset) and the Front of his Stoor being inspected by Patrolmen.

The police also considered that the incident could have been a prank by one of the bus passengers, who fired a gun from the inside. However, examination of the bullet hole proved that the shot was fired from the outside of the bus. However, in spite of this fact, and simply because they could find no other explanation, a few investigators held to the belief that the shot was fired from the inside. This notion would soon be disproven when the mysterious attacks continued.

The next attack occurred the following day on January 25th, when a shop on Cramer Hill came under fire. Papers excitedly reported on the return of Camden's "phantom sniper" and wrote that "using the same mysterious method as that employed by the unknown gunner who has shot holes in the windshields of five automobiles and a motorbus in the last few weeks, someone yesterday fired a missile through the plate glass door at a store conducted by Gottlob Mayer."

Again, no bullet was found at the scene, nor was a gunshot heard. The paper wrote that "authorities investigating the incidents have been faced with the additional problem of attempting to discover the nature of a missile which to all intents and purposes, disappears as though into thin air after striking."

As media reports of the strange projectiles gained more traction, what may have been a copycat incident was perpetrated. At 4:45 A.M. on January 28th, a tall, shadowy looking man fired a bullet through the bedroom window of two girls. He ran off after one of the girls spied him from their window, and one of the girls heard him say, "It's all right now, Louie!" as he ran off. This time a lead bullet was found at the scene, so there was nothing supernatural about that occurrence. The papers also noted that the bullet was "no blue marble" this time. They also made note that it was unusual in this case that a bullet was found since before the projectiles seemed to vanish.

However, the same morning, the phantom gunman had recently assaulted a trolley car. The case was identical in circumstance to that of the bus from earlier in that no shot was heard and no bullet was found.

THAT PHANTOM SNIPER

A Collingswood Mail Bagger suggests the Phantom Sniper is nothing but a series of pebbles chancing to be thrown by the tires of passing cars against the windshields of other cars. The theory is ingenious, and in a way plausible, but it simply won't do for such a series of incidents as has been reported. So many repetitions involve more than a reasonable amount of coincidence.

First place, a pebble thus snapped by a tire shoots out SIDEWAYS. It would not hit straight against a windshield coming toward it, with bullet force. The blow would be glancing.

The stories take more definite form with the report of two girls having seen the Phantom Sniper. A bullet was sent through their bedroom window. And the bullet was found. Thus the story is removed from the realms of romantic fancy.

Five windshields, on private cars; one bus windshield, a store window, and a trolley car window. That is the sniper's score to date.

"I didn't know what happened," the driver told the paper. "I heard the bullet strike the window and I heard it sing as it passed by my head and go into the interior of the car. I saw no one who might have fired the shot."

With nearly a dozen shootings under his belt, the "phantom sniper" had become public enemy number one in Camden.

Captain of Detectives John Golden said that he would "detail several plain clothes men immediately to run down this half-wit and take him into custody before he kills somebody."

On January 28th a man identified only by his initials, H.M.R., wrote to the *Camden-Courier Post* to tell the editor that he too had a plate glass window shot through in Camden. In this case, he found a small rock fragment. He speculated that perhaps a passing motor had propelled it through the window. In his humble opinion, the pebbles were the answer to the mystery—except that they weren't.

The next incident had another windshield shot out with disappearing bullets of which there was no trace. As the media frenzy continued over the sniper, it would seem that many people began blaming the phantom sniper on all kinds of crimes. A drive-by shooting was attributed to the sniper on January 30th (.22 bullets were found at the scene of the crime in this case). One man, ashamed to admit that he accidentally shot himself blamed it on the phantom sniper. Two men up to no good and injured in an explosion claimed that their burns came from the phantom sniper! (In the interest of being thorough, though, it was never proven either way what happened in that case.) Next, there was a problematic "phantom witness," which was possibly a hoax.

A "Harry F. Cheeseman of Magnolia [Road]" breathlessly pulled up to the Camden police station and claimed that he had been fired upon by the Phantom Sniper (driving a vehicle this time). However, later attempts to track down this man proved that he had used a false name. The real Mr. Cheeseman claimed he hadn't even been out of the house the day that the man using his name went to the police.

It gets murkier from there, as a projectile screw was fired through a window a bit later. So again, in addition to the mostly invisible bullets had been found a blue marble, a few .22s, and now a screw. While these incidents were odd but still explainable, the vanishing bullets returned on February 5th, when they drilled their way through an auto traveling along the Crescent Road.

On Cooper Street a missile shot through the front window of a car driven by Bruce Wallace, a former high school athlete/local celebrity. Coincidentally, Wallace worked in the offices of Albert S. Woodruff, the sniper's very first victim. The paper wrote that the bullet Wallace experienced "vanished into thin air." Just like the bus driver some weeks ago, Wallace said he heard no gunshot, but a "whining noise." Suddenly a hole pierced his windshield and that was that.

Adding to the chaos, that same day, two small boys in another locale decided to play "phantom sniper" for themselves. They shot their BB guns at a passing train and were later taken into custody by the police.

Target No. 18

BRUCE "PARRY" WALLACE
Former star athlete of Camden High School, who was the eighteenth target of Camden's "phantom sniper." He was driving his car on Cooper street when one of the mysterious marksman's "disappearing bullets" drilled through the windshield of the auto.

The same night as Wallace's experience, along the same road, was traveling James Paharazyn. He reportedly either saw the mystery projectile in this instance or felt it pass by. An article published in the *Courier* on February 6th quoted Pharazyn as stating the following. "Something whizzed past in front of me and struck a house, just over my head. It made a hole in the wall of the house like a bullet might have done. I didn't hear any explosion or the report of a gun."

The projectiles continued to baffle police, as they were unaware of any gun in existence that could produce such holes with no noise. One article published on the 7th wrote that, "The Philadelphia Rapid Transit Company is making experiments with various guns and bullets in an effort to find a weapon which would make a hole similar to the one fired by the sniper."

This image shows patrolman Arthur Cosley holding one of six newly acquired machine guns that the police had purchased to deal with the Phantom.

Leon Furman, another victim of the sniper, shows where an invisible bullet pierced his window in the paper on February 9th

The February 9th *Courier* reported on another disturbing incident. William Turnbull had just sat down to do some reading in front of a window in his home. It was 9 P.M. and a shade was drawn over the window. Suddenly, the glass shattered, but no gunshot was heard. Turnbull, when he felt it was safe, examined the window. He was shocked to find a hole six inches in diameter. Stranger yet, whatever pierced the window did not affect the shade at all. It was undamaged. Once again, no bullet was ever found.

Turnbull told police that shortly before the glass exploded he heard a car stop near his home, and he also heard the car door open and shut. Suspiciously, it also drove away after the glass broke. However, this is purely circumstantial evidence. No one saw any shooters. Furthermore, police found no footprints outside in the "moist earth" of Turnbull's lawn. And yes, they scoured the ground for the projectile and still found nothing.

The next day, the *Evening Courier* and *Morning Post* of Camden pooled their resources to offer a $500 reward to anyone who could prove the existence or lead to the capture of the Phantom. The papers received a slew of letters offering theories as to either who the phantom was, or what he was using. The event was an interesting precursor to the letters that flooded newspapers during the saga of the famous Zodiac killer in the late 1960s and early 1970s. Like the Phantom Sniper, that case is still unsolved to this day. Similar to people who wrote in claiming to know the Zodiac, at least one anonymous letter told the police where and when they could find the shooter. The writer warned them not to publish the letter so as to tip off the sniper. The letter ended ominously "Till we meet again, Captain" and was signed, simply "a gunman." The tip as to where and when to find the sniper naturally turned out not to be true.

On February 9th, the sniper fired their 21st shot into another Camden business. Again, no bullet could be found. The 25th "ghost bullet" was fired into a taxi cab on the 10th.

Truck Driver Nathan Brodsky poses for the paper to show the entry point of the invisible bullet that pierced his truck on February 11th

The next bizarre occurrence again added to and confused the mythos of the phantom sniper. A man named George Murphy was driving a truck behind some sort of unspecified automobile on the road. Suddenly, Murphy's windshield was penetrated by an invisible bullet. He attributed it to the men in the vehicle in front of him. He claimed that they suspiciously looked back at him often. Furthermore, the exhaust pipe on their car curved upward to an unusual extent, suggesting it had been modified. He believed the strange exhaust pipe was really a special air gun! Again, that's his own theory and the odd exhaust pipes could be purely circumstantial.

On February 13th the *Courier* reported that the police had received another letter signed "a gunman." This letter named the shooter as 21-year-old Eugene Marshall. When asked about it by the police, Marshall denied the accusation and accused the writer of the letter as being the actual phantom trying to put the blame on him!

What's more, Marshall felt he knew who it was. The letter once again ended with the closing statement of "'til we meet again." Marshall claimed that this is what the man he suspected wrote the letter said to him the last time he saw him. Nothing ever came of the letters, by the way, they were just another tantalizing loose end in the investigation.

The phantom shootings and copycats continued. Just days after a young boy was playing "phantom shooter" and shot his bb gun through a school window, a real phantom sniper school shooting occurred. Only one shot was fired through the glass window of the schoolroom and the terrified children took cover. The teacher saw a car driving away when she looked out the window and assumed that perhaps it carried the shooter. Once again, no bullet was ever found.

Later that night, on the 16th, a bus driver taking a bus out on a test drive was assaulted by a man in a Ford motor car. This time he saw a gun being pointed at him. The assailant shot at him, broke the glass, and sped off. A blue marble was found, just like the one that hit the police officer back in January.

Three other shootings were recorded that night. But there was no car associated with them. At 3:30 A.M. three homes had a projectile fired through their windows. No blue marbles were found this time. No projectile at all was found at any of the three sites, nor was a car associated with those three incidents. So, the instance of the man firing on the bus could have been another copycat, perhaps one who read about the blue marble some time ago?

The shootings continued to confuse. On February 22nd the papers reported how a projectile breached the window of a local store. The hole it made was too small for either a bullet, a marble, or a pebble. The store owner heard nothing but the impact itself. He went outside and reported smelling smoke. Two small boys were in the vicinity, and when he asked them if they had seen anything they said no but that they heard something whizz by their heads.

That day an 18-year-old named Hyman Tucker was arrested under suspicion that he was the sniper. That night, while he was in custody, the sniper struck again. A hole no bigger than a matchstick was created by an invisible missile that sailed through a truck's front window.

The phantom sniper hit his 50th target in the form of the car of Louis Ware, the "Asparagus King of South Jersey." At noon on the 23rd the sniper hit another bus. Appropriately, the sniper's final shot was fired into a car dealership. It happened on either the 23rd or 24th of February. Curiously, the shot that made the hole was noiseless. But, a few moments later, three mystery gunshots were heard with no discernable source.

A green car drove by which the witnesses assumed might be the shooter. Suspiciously, it turned out its headlights and sped off. Police searched for the vehicle but found nothing. And that was the last anyone ever heard of the "phantom sniper," whose identity is unknown to this day. If said sniper has an identity, that is, which brings us to our next point of discussion.

Remember the man who theorized that pebbles were to blame? Well, what if those pebbles were actually space slag? George Mitrovic, author of *UFOs – An Atlas and History, 1800-1977*, puts forth the fascinating theory that Camden wasn't under siege by a phantom sniper, but a mini-cosmic dust storm of sorts.

His idea isn't unfounded. In the history of humankind, only two people have ever been struck by slag that we know of. Both were women living in Alabama 50 years apart. What strange odds, and why Alabama of all places on Earth? Who knows, but Flagstaff, Arizona, where the Great Meteor crater sits, in particular is subject to a higher than normal amount of meteors than anywhere else. Not just prehistoric ones, like the Barringer Meteor

Crater, but meteor craters created across several different time periods dot Arizona. Overall, there are 28 craters in the state. Now, meteors should, and usually do, strike the earth erratically rather than hitting the same spots over and over again.

Mitrovic theorized that perhaps, for several months, somehow an Oort Cloud bombarded Camden. And what is an Ort Cloud, you ask? It's made up of icy particles of space debris. Theoretically, let's say one streaked through the atmosphere just long enough to puncture a window, and then the remains melted. This would account for the "invisible bullets." As to how they would hit the same spots as Earth revolved, Mitrovic put forth the idea that perhaps a mini-wormhole existed that somehow transported the fragments to Camden. As to instances where a man or a boy was sighted with a gun, those could easily be labeled as copycats, mimicking what the press dubbed a shooter, but was in fact a cosmic dust storm of sorts. Again, that's just one theory. A theory that's made all the harder to swallow by the fact that occasionally screws, marbles and bullets were found at the crime scenes.

And yet, despite the occasional projectile that was found, they were very rare. Of the over 50 recorded shooting, usually no projectile was ever found. The occasional blue marble or screw, if anything, seemed like a cruel joke on investigators. And again, no bullet of any kind could account for the curious, near microscopic points of entry of some of the holes.

Paranormal investigator Charles Fort, in his book *Wild Talents*, said, "Authorities in Jersey towns, noting the range of the malefactor, were especially watchful of motorists: but it is my notion that he had no need for anything on wheels in which to do his traveling." Unfortunately, Fort doesn't elaborate upon his cryptic comment, but we took it to mean Fort felt something supernatural was afoot.

Good ol' Fort also dug up an earlier phantom sniper account, also from New Jersey (in Glassboro). It also occurred in the month of February, but in the year 1916. It was only one instance in this case, but it was identical to the Camden case in that a silent, invisible bullet sailed through a window and into a house, never to be found. The papers dubbed them "phantom bullets" in 1916. The fact that it took place in February may not just be a coincidence. For instance, did you know that you are more likely to see a UFO on June 24th (St. John's Day) than any other day in the year? And yes, that was the day of Kenneth Arnold's landmark sighting in 1947. As researchers who studied the data found, that day typically has more UFO sightings across history compared to any other day. So, that the Phantom Sniper appeared in the month of February could be telling.

Along that same whimsical line of thought, there is a chance that the "Cosmic Sniper" was a form of extraterrestrial. Not just any extraterrestrial, though, but a true cosmic practical joker. John Keel called such entities "ultraterrestrials"— interdimensional beings that were possibly the inspirations for the trickster gods of old, like Loki, the Norse god of mischief. Among their kin were the mischievous "little people," be they fairies or aliens (who share more traits than you might think).

Keel's idea, percolating in his head for many years, came to fruition in the form of his book *Disneyland of the Gods.* In the book, he suggested that all of our great mysteries that made no sense were orchestrated by superior beings for their own demented amusement. Keel wasn't the only paranormal investigator who thought along these lines. The great naturalist/cryptozoologist/ufologist Ivan Sanderson came to a similar but more chilling belief in the 1960s. He believed that the Earth was essentially a farm for the E.T.'s, and we were the livestock (the implication there not being that man was created by the E.T.'s, just that we were powerless against their visits and experimentation the same way that a cow is powerless and against a human). Charles Fort in collecting what he called his "damned data" also hinted that something sinister sat at the middle of life's great mysteries. He once wrote that "I think we are property. Someone owns this earth. All others warned off."

To return to Keel's ultra-terrestrial practical joke theory, the phantom sniper fits the concept perfectly. The contradictory evidence in the case certainly seems as though it's a cosmic joke on the human race. Predominantly, in most accounts of the Phantom Sniper, no shots were heard, no bullets were found, and no shooters were seen. That was the norm for the case. What was unusual was when the projectiles were found, or when a shooter was seen.

Also alluding to a cosmic joke is the phantom witness "Harry F. Cheeseman of Magnolia Road." Some Fortean researchers consider the word Magnolia to be interchangeable with the word Magonia, the name given to a mythical realm where fairies dwelled. The great Jacques Vallee wrote the book *Passport to Magonia*, which compared modern UFO visitations to mystical encounters with fairies and mythical beings of yore. Perhaps the phantom witness from Magnolia was really alluding to Magonia? It was this witness who confused matters by adding in a new element to the case, that the phantom sniper drove a car. More alarming than the "Magnolia Road" connection were the three shootings that took place at 3:30 A.M. on February 16th. Though most laymen assume that the "witching hour" is at midnight, it is actually at 3:30 A.M. More paranormal encounters—be they with aliens, cryptids, or ghosts—take place at that time of night/early morning than at any other time. That the cosmic sniper perpetrated a triple hit at that hour is eyebrow raising indeed.

To attempt a conclusion to this thoroughly winding rabbit hole we've just dived down, we have three explanations on the table. One, the shooter was a rather exceptional individual in possession of a strange air gun with the ability to fire screws, marbles, and other projectiles that could never be found. (Though technically within the realm of possibility, this idea seems nearly as fishy as the other three.)

Two, Camden is one of those special areas, like Arizona, that for a time was the recipient of a special cosmic shower of some sort. This shower began the myth of the Phantom Sniper, which in turn spawned copycats, accounting for the very rare sighting of a man firing a gun.

Three, the Phantom Sniper was some type of extraterrestrial or interdimensional entity - a cosmic practical joker that left behind just enough evidence to madden and confuse investigators.

Do aliens or interdimensional beings occasionally pop up to play tricks on the human race? It may sound far out, but cases like the "Phantom Sniper" of Camden, New Jersey, are just whacky enough to make one consider the theory.

35

THE STAR THAT SPLIT IN TWO

New York, New York
March 1928

ASTRONOMERS RECIEVED a shock in March 1928 when a star that had just been discovered in 1925 suddenly split into two. The event caught the attention of pioneering paranormal researcher Charles Fort, who mocked astronomers for having observed the star and photographed it for 25 years before realizing what it was. Then, when it suddenly split in two, the learned men once again seemed powerless to explain what had happened.

An article in the *Press and Sun Bulletin* of Binghamton, New York, on March 30, 1928 said,

"Astronomers who are studying the heavens report that the star Nova Pictoris has cataclysmically divided and become two stars. If this report is true, it is an astronomical phenomenon of universal interest."

Democrat and Chronicle (Rochester, N.Y), May 6, 1928, p. 66

An article in the Rochester, New York, *Democrat and Chronicle* on May 6, 1928, said, "Whether Nova Pictoris, first observed by Earth astronomers three years ago, has been rent in twain by internal explosion or wrecked in collision with another astral body is big puzzle now engaging the attention of our star gazers."

South African astronomer W. H. van den Bos wrote, "In March of that year [1925], Mr. [William S.] Finsen ... made an amazing discovery: the nova looked like a close double star, involved in nebulosity. This was so unprecedented that, after Finsen's observation had been confirmed the next night by Dr. [Robert] Innes and myself and the news had been cabled to the astronomical world, it was met with marked skepticism and incredulity."

THE STAR THAT HAS SPLIT IN TWO

Astronomers who are studying the heavens report that the star Nova Pictoris has cataclysmically divided and become two stars.

If this report is true, it is an astronomical phenomenon of universal interest.

When Nova Pictoris split it is possible it may have involved the death and the annihilation of a solar system of worlds similar to our own.

Astronomers differ in their conclusions in regard to this splitting of Nova Pictoris. Dr. Luyten of Harvard University says that the phenomenon observed may have been the mere coming into view of a hitherto unobserved companion of the star affected. No one on this earth ever saw Nova Pictoris, so far as astronomical records go, until 1925. It is impossible to see it without a powerful telescope.

Although some observers suspected the splitting of the star into two stars had a paranormal angle to it in 1925, history seems to dispute that it was anything out of the ordinary. Astronomers now say that Nova Pictoris is actually a double star, comprised of a white dwarf and a secondary star that is so close that the two bodies exchange stellar material. At various times during the exchange of material, the material will ignite and significantly increase the brightness of the star system.

The two stars of Nova Pictoris orbit each other every 3.48 hours. They are approximately 1,700 light years away from our planet.

In the end, although this strange astronomical phenomenon did pique the interest of Charles Fort and other paranormal researchers, it was nonetheless a normal, albeit fascinating, natural event.

36
GIANT UFO OVER MIAMI

Miami, Florida
June 13, 1928

ON JUNE 13, 1928, at about 9 p.m., a bizarre aerial phenomenon appeared directly over Miami, Florida and persisted for more than thirty minutes, while thousands of the city's residents cowered in awe and fear.

An enormous light that some described as "like a comet without a tail" suddenly flickered on in the sky above the city. *The Miami News* said, "A strange body of light appeared overhead, like a full moon seen through misty clouds. It became visible suddenly, as if someone had turned on a huge frosted electric bulb...."

MIAMI ASTRONOMERS UNABLE TO IDENTIFY PHENOMENON IN SKY

Enormous Light, Resembled Comet, Is Not Believed To Be One.

The Miami (Fla.) Herald, 6-14-1928, p. 1.

Miami's other newspaper, *The Herald*, said, "In appearance, it resembled a great blurred electric light." The size of the object was "several hundred times" the size of nearby stars in the night sky.

Amateur astronomer Robert C. Fahrion said, "Because of its great size, I am certain that it was not a star distorted by mist in our atmosphere."

Miami astronomers were trying to decide last night and this morning the classification of a phenomenon which appeared in Miami skies, directly overhead, last night.

The phenomenon, closely resembling a tailless comet, was visible for more than 30 minutes between 9 p. m. and 10 p. m. It appeared to be several hundred times the size of nearby stars.

In appearance it resembled a great blurred electric light. Mrs. Eddy Starr, 526 S. E. Tenth avenue, who observed it throughout its appearance, said that after 20 minutes or so it took on some color, much like the colors of a rainbow, but these resolved themselves again into the blurred gray.

The phenomenon contracted and disappeared quite suddenly. R. C. Fahrion, 711 S. W. Fifth avenue, an astronomer of note, observed the phenomenon without his telescope for a short time, but it disappeared while he was setting up his glass.

"It had every appearance of a comet, except that it had no tail," he said. "I do not believe it was a comet, since one of that size would have been listed and we would have had word of its coming. In addition this thing did not move and it disappeared too suddenly. It was of such enormous size that if it had appeared before it should have been studied and recorded.

"Because of its great size I am certain that it was not a star distorted by mist in our atmosphere. It may be we will hear something more about it later from someone elsewhere, or from some large observatory that had a glass trained on it. It has me stumped."

James J. Marshall, secretary of the Southern Cross Observatory, which operates in Royal Palm park during the winter, did not see the phenomenon. He said that sometimes mist in the earth's atmosphere will cause unusual astronomical appearances. The reported size of this phenomenon, he said, makes it wise to await reports from large observatories and astronomical magazines before drawing conclusions.

The Miami (Fla.) Herald, 6-14-1928, p. 1.

At first, the bright light hovering over the city was just an intense white in color. However, after about 20 minutes, colors began to appear, similar to the colors of a rainbow. As more time passed, the colors faded into a blurry gray.

Although some described it as a "tailless comet," astronomers seemed certain that it was not a comet at all. "None of the large observatories, where a constant watch for such appearances is kept, knew anything of the occurrence, so far as could be learned," said the *Miami News*. Meanwhile, Fahrion said, "I do not believe it was a comet, since one of that size would have been listed, and we would have had word of its coming. In addition, this thing did not move, and it disappeared too suddenly. It was of such enormous size that if it had appeared before [in history], it should have been studied and recorded."

Fahrion added that he was "stumped" by the strange apparition. "It may be we will hear something more about it later from someone elsewhere or from some large observatory that had a glass trained on it." Fahrion had attempted to retrieve his telescope in time to view the object, but it had vanished before he could set it up.

Also greatly mystified by the reported size of the phenomenon was James J. Marshall, secretary of the Miami-based Southern Cross Observatory, an organization of amateur astronomers.

According to the 1930 U.S. Census, Robert C. Fahrion lived in Miami and was 52 years old in 1928. His occupation is listed as "photographer," working at a "photography studio." James J. Marshall, 38 years old in 1928, is listed in the census as an attorney living in Miami.

An interesting aspect of this case is that the phenomenon was only seen over Miami. Also, it does not appear from the historical record that scientists ever came up with a theory as to the cause of the apparition. Finally, the massive object was perfectly stationary over the city for over 30 minutes. As far as UFO researchers are concerned, the phenomenon is best explained as a city-sized extraterrestrial spacecraft hovering over Miami!

37

UFO STOPS CAR

Near Tulsa, Oklahoma
August 1928

A LETTER FROM a reader in the October 1973 edition of *Fate* magazine disclosed a fascinating UFO encounter from August 1928 near Tulsa, Oklahoma.

Aaron C. Stern, the eyewitness, and his father were driving from their home in Tulsa to Norman, Oklahoma – a journey of about 120 miles. They left Tulsa before dawn in their Willys Knight automobile.

Stern said, "Our Willys Knight car was performing smoothly until we were about fifty miles west of Tulsa when it started to miss and backfire. I suspected dirt in the fuel line and as the motor coughed and died, I coasted to the shoulder of the road and stopped. Dad suggested that the filter might be dirty and that I should clean that first."

1928 Willys Knight
(by By Niels de Wit from Lunteren, The Netherlands)

CC BY 2.0, https://commons.wikimedia.org/w/index.php?curid=37747933

Although neither man was very adept at roadside repairs, Stern opened the car's hood and hoped to be able to do something to get the car back up and running.

Stern said, "As I started to look under the hood, suddenly the whole area was illuminated by the brightest light I have ever seen. It flashed by, about 150 feet overhead. It was primarily a white light but as it faded it seemed to burst into many colors like a fireworks spectacle. Then darkness closed in again."

Artist's Simulation (Pixabay)

The two men stood speechless for a few moments, and then, they both blurted out almost simultaneously, "What was that?"

"For the next 15 to 30 minutes we stood there trying to understand what had occurred. No other traffic passed and as the first light of dawn began to break we were able to determine there were no farmhouses nearby – just open country. There were no clues to explain this puzzling phenomenon."

Nothing under the hood seemed amiss, and the gas filter was not dirty. Stern decided to try restarting the engine, and it immediately started, enabling them to resume their trip to Norman.

Later, Stern and his father did some checking with local authorities in an effort to determine what the strange object they saw might have been. "The county sheriff, the highway patrol, newspaper editors and several astronomers from larger observatories could give us no explanation for the occurrence. I can only conclude it was a 1928 UFO."

38

LITTLE BLONDE MEN FROM SATURN

Lake Geneva, Wisconsin
October 15, 1928

ON AUGUST 30, 1955, an article in the *Cincinnati (Ohio) Enquirer* daily newspaper disclosed a bizarre "flying saucer" story that happened in 1928, when the eyewitness was a young woman. The story was told by a Cincinnati nurse named Velma Thayer, who owned a farm near Lake Geneva, Wisconsin. The article was written up by highly respected newspaper reporter Jack Ramey (1908-1963).

Thayer stated that a small flying saucer landed on her farm on October 15, 1928, and the strange ship remained there for ten days. As she approached the saucer, she saw several "little men" step out of the ship. The little humanoids were between four feet and five feet in height and had blond hair.

The Planet Saturn (NASA Photo)

Thayer stated that one of the strangers was able to communicate with her, gave his name as "Ramu," and claimed that he and his party were from Saturn. He told her that he and the others have come to Earth on a completely peaceful mission. They said to her that they had a "protective interest" in our planet and that they would take steps to protect Earth from unspecified "dangers."

Ramu told her that the little flying saucer in which he had arrived was merely a "scout ship" and that his people had a large "mother ship" far out in space. The mother ship carried as many as 100 of the scout ships and was between 16 and 60 miles in length.

Thayer was also told that the visitors had a special means of communication like "their own telephone system." Even after the little men had departed, Thayer said she could still contact them using their phone system, although she did not explain how it worked.

Charles F. Kettering

As previously noted, the flying saucer remained landed on her farm for ten days, during which it was visited by at least one member of the U.S. military, a scientist named Charles F. Kettering, and a

Phillip K. Wrigley

famous Chicago businessman, Phillip K. Wrigley.

Kettering (1876-1958), an Ohio native, was an inventor, engineer, businessman, and the holder of 186 U.S. patents for his inventions. He was the head of research at General Motors from 1920 to 1947.

Little Men, Saucer, Remained 10 Days?

VELMA THAYER, a Cincinnati nurse, 2514 Ingleside Ave., is going to sit down with me in a cemetery or other isolated place sometime in the future and tell me the saucer men's protective interest in the earth.

This is not a laughing matter with Velma Thayer.

She owns a farm near Lake Geneva, Wis. She remembers well a flying saucer landing there, October 15, 1928, and remaining for 10 days.

She greeted the little men courteously, not little green men, but blond little fellows four feet six to five feet three inches in height. She only was able to establish communications with one little man, named **Ramu**, from Saturn.

She remembers that **Charles Kettering** from Kettering Laboratories and **Phil Wrigley**, the chewing gum scion, saw the space ship after a U. S. guard had been placed upon it. She remembers that the flying saucer was there, being inspected, for 10 days — until the guard fell asleep. Whoosh, away went the flying saucer with its little men.

The thing was that Ramu told her the flying saucer was merely a scout ship from a mother ship far out in space; that the mother ships were 16 to 60 miles in length and that the largest "mother" could harbor as many as 100 flying saucers.

Another thing is that the little men convinced her, through Ramu, that their intentions were completely peaceful. From what do the little men wish to protect the earth? Velma Thayer will tell me, she said, when we sit down together in that cemetery or other isolated place.

The little men possess their own telephone system and she is in contact with them at odd times.

Meantime, Velma Thayer said, she and the Ketterings and the Wrigleys wanted no more to do about the whole thing.

* * *

*The Cincinnati Enquirer
(Cincinnati, Ohio),
Aug. 30, 1955, p. 5*

Wrigley (1894-1977) was an American chewing gum manufacturer and professional baseball executive. He was the son of William Wrigley, Jr., the founder of the Wrigley Chewing Gum Company and owner of the Chicago Cubs professional baseball team.

Unfortunately, Thayer never explained why, of all the important persons in the United States in 1928, only Kettering and Wrigley came to look at the landed UFO.

The last part of the story is even more bizarre and a bit difficult to understand. Thayer stated that the military placed a guard at the landing site to watch the saucer at all times, but that one night, the soldier fell asleep while on duty. As the guard slept, "Whoosh, away went the flying saucer with its little men," Thayer said.

Newspaper reporter Jack Ramey, who did general reporting and writing for the *Cincinnati Enquirer* from 1937 until his death in 1963, was known to sometimes tackle "controversial" topics, and his article about Thayer certainly qualifies. Ramey died of cancer in 1963 at age 55, and Thayer is believed to have died in 1977.

Image from Piqsels.com

39

UFO STARTLES CATTLE

Milton, North Dakota
November 1928

EARLY IN NOVEMBER 1928, 12-year-old
Norman H. Sabie and his brother, Thorsten, were
on horseback on a ranch located four miles
northeast of Milton, North Dakota, when they
witnessed something that would remain with them
for the rest of their lives.

Streaking out of the northern sky with a
tremendous roar came a UFO that looked like a
round, silver-colored "inverted soup bowl." It was
flying extremely low, no more than 15 or 20 feet
above the ground. "Almost at eye level," Sabie later
said.

The shiny flying disc had a "hump" in the center and had four beams of light shining down from the front part of the craft, aimed at Sabie and his brother. The effect of the lights on the surrounding landscape was "ghostly."

The craft appeared to be made of smooth, shiny metal, silver in color. It was approximately 20 to 25 feet in diameter. The sound emanating from it seemed to diminish a bit.

The strange craft approached to within 100 to 150 feet of the two horsemen, moving extremely quickly. "The speed was unearthly," Sabie said.

The two brothers fought to control their herd of frightened cattle, spooked by the UFO's loud noise "like air coming out of a vacuum cleaner."

UFO (Image by Peter Lomas from Pixabay)

The entire transit of the craft, from the time they spotted it until it zoomed past them and vanished off to the south, lasted a total of about 10 to 15 seconds.

Historical documents confirm that Norman H. Sabie was born in Fairdale, North Dakota, on September 28, 1916. He later moved to LaPorte, Indiana, where he lived for 51 years and worked at Grandorf Plumbing & Heating for 34 years.

After disclosing his encounter, Sabie was interviewed by investigators from the National Investigations Committee on Aerial Phenomena (NICAP). The investigators also spoke to persons who knew the witness. The picture that emerged was that Sabie was "honest, upright, truthful ... good moral character and well-liked and respected man in the community."

In his book *Mysteries of the Skies: UFOs in Perspective* (1968), UFO investigator Gordon I.R. Lore assessed the case, writing, "In the interview in which he described the sighting, Sable's answers were quick and firm, with a minimum of speculation and no apparent embellishment. With surprising understatement, Sabie described his overall reaction as 'startled.' When asked if he thought the craft might have been guided by intelligence, he answered, 'It had to be.'"

Sabie passed away on January 31, 1995, at the age of 78, in LaPorte, Indiana.

Sawmill at Ward's Cove April 1929

40

UFO OVER SAWMILL

Ward, Colorado
April 1929

✦

SIMILAR TO THE 1927 photo of a UFO in Oregon, the picture to be discussed in this chapter appears to be authentic and seems to show a technologically advanced metallic saucer flying over the town of Ward, Colorado in April 1929.

The photo was submitted to UFO researchers by Hetty Pline, along with this brief explanation: "This photo was taken by my father Edward Pline at the sawmill in Ward where we lived at the time, I think it was 1929. I was about six years old then. My father was there to photograph the sawmill for some reason or another, and as he was taking the photo, he described a 'terrible thunderous below,' and a large round thing as big as a very large boulder that moved through the air above them."

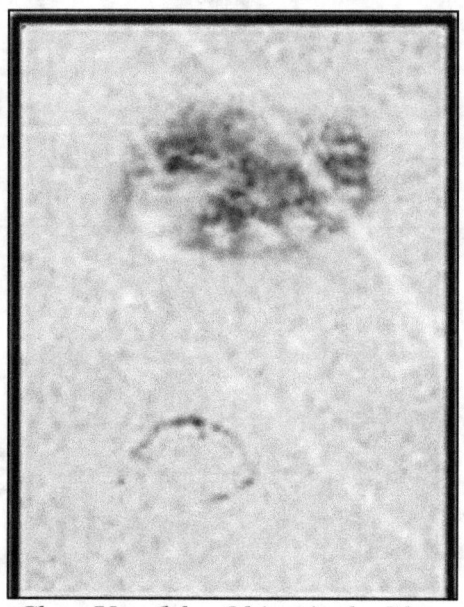

Close Up of the Object in the Photo

Hetty Pline also said, "You can see it in the picture. None of the sawmill workers saw the thing in the photo, but they all heard the sound and felt the ground shudder. Later in my life I tried researching the incident at the County Historical Society, but I did not find any references to it. My father passed on a few years after the incident, and I have not found any surviving sawmill workers from that time. Perhaps you have more information about this incident."

In a close up of the strange object in the sky, we can see what is a dark saucer-shape with a row of portals or windows visible on the lower part of the shape. There are also two points on the saucer that could be protrusions. They are blurry masses – a larger one on the upper right and a smaller one on the lower left. Interestingly, there is also a semi-circular artifact in the sky below and to the left of the UFO. It almost seems like a reflection or perhaps some type of wake or propulsion signature.

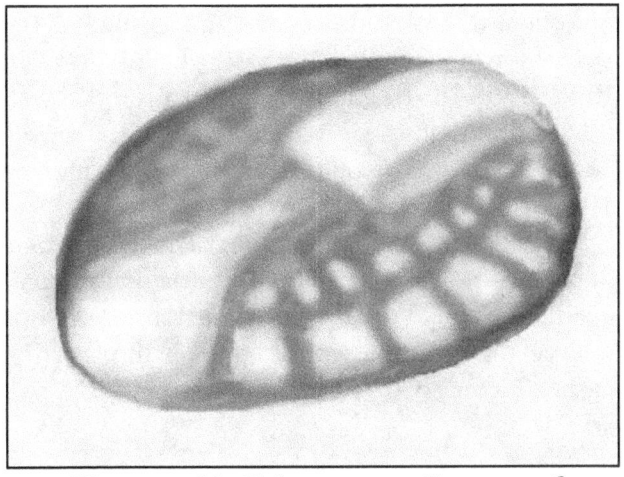

Photographic Enhancement Courtesy of
UFOevidence.org

In an analysis posted on *UFOevidence.org,* the late UFO researcher Earl J. Neff (1902-1993) commented on a photographic enhancement of the main object. Neff said, "This illustrative enhancement was produced by enlarging the image and overpainting the various values present, while flattening the high grain distortion in the image and eliminating scratches on the film."

Interestingly, the enhancement provided by Neff seems to show a more "organic" object, almost like a turtle shell, rather than something that is clearly a machine. It almost seems like some kind of strange, giant flying turtle along the lines of the fictional Gamera in Japanese *kaiju* films.

The location where this UFO photograph was taken has an interesting history. It was established in 1860 after the discovery of gold at nearby Gold Hill. Ward, Colorado, ended up as one of the richest towns in the state during the Colorado Gold Rush (1858-1861). After the gold was tapped out, the town went into steep decline. The 1920 census counted only 74 people living in Ward, and by 1930, the number was down to just 34.

What the object in the photo actually was may never be known. It remains an intriguing mystery even today. Like the Oregon Junction photo, it is one of the most intriguing UFO pictures of the early 20th century.

UFO LANDING

Burns, Oregon
July 5, 1929

FOR MANY YEARS, the National UFO Reporting Center (NUFORC) has allowed members of the public to report UFO sightings by phone or, more recently, via their website, *nuforc.org.* The organization, begun in 1974, has catalogued almost 90,000 reported UFO sightings over its history, mostly from the United States. While most reports submitted to NUFORC are about recent sightings, a few are about cases that occurred many, many years prior.

On July 31, 2002, NUFORC received a report that was submitted anonymously regarding an amazing up-close UFO encounter that happened on July 5, 1929 at approximately 2 p.m. near Burns, Oregon.

1930 Photo Taken in Burns, Oregon
(Oregon State Univ. Archives)

The witness reported that the sighting occurred while he and his mother were travelling by automobile from Burns, Oregon, toward the nearby town of Hines, located about 3 miles southeast of Burns. The witness said, "We were traveling east of Burns [Oregon], climbing up through a cut in the rim rocks, when this object [UFO] very slowly flew over the top of us, some fifty feet above the rim rock."

The object was about 100 yards in length, brown in color and had windows along its hull. It came to a stationary hovering position nearby as the eyewitness stopped the car and pulled over for a closer look. It made a soft humming noise as it hovered. "The object stopped, and through the [leftmost] window, there were two beings, looked most like our type of people. I could see them pointing with arms and hands."

Artist's Rendition of UFO
(Image by CoolCatGameStudio from Pixabay)

The comment that the UFO occupants were "like our type of people," is significant in indicating these were humanoids with no features that seemed immediately unusual.

"I stepped out of the car, but my mother demanded that I get back into the car. I stood on the running board the rest of the short time." From these comments, we learn that the rest of the observation, which was about one minute in total, was made by the witness while standing on the running board outside his car. Clearly, his mother, still sitting inside the car, was terrified at what she saw and continued to insist that the witness return to the relative safety of the vehicle.

"The craft was two tones [shades] of brown. It hovered for about 40 seconds. The craft had windows in the middle section. There was a soft hum. You could [not] detect any movement, or vibration of any kind."

Suddenly, the UFO began to move, very slowly at first, away from the area. "As it left, it moved very slowly. One of the persons walked to the next window. About that is when they started to move the craft. [It] must have been somewhere at 100 yards in length, because you could not quite see total length. Then in a blink, it was gone."

After the strange object had disappeared, the witness's mother turned to him and said, "Don't say anything about this, because people will think we are crazy."

THE COLDWATER INCIDENT

Off the Coast of Virginia
August 29, 1929

ON AUGUST 29, 1929, the steamship *Coldwater*, located about 400 miles off the coast of Virginia, spotted an amazing sight overhead – a large, mysterious airship moving at about 100 miles per hour in the general direction of Bermuda. No explanation for this mysterious sighting was ever uncovered, as pointed out by paranormal researcher Charles Fort in his book *Lo!*

An article published in the September 3, 1929 edition of the *Chattanooga (Tennessee) Daily Times* said, "A vivid account of an unidentified airplane, sighted last Thursday night winging its way across the north Atlantic about 400 miles off the Virginia capes, was given today upon arrival here of the steamship Coldwater, of the South Atlantic Steamship line.

Typical Steamship of the Period (Wikipedia)

"Members of the crew told of the sighting of the plane, as related to them by Tom Stuart, third mate of the Coldwater, who was on watch at the time and was the only man aboard to see the adventurous flyer.

"According to Stuart's report, the plane was headed in the direction of Europe in the teeth of a gale which was sweeping along at a rate, estimated by the ships officers, at more than 100 miles an hour. Owing to the force of the gale It was impossible for Stuart to hear the engine, so he could not determine whether the plane was of the single or tri-motored type. From the lights in the cabin, however, Stuart told the crew he gained the impression that it was a large passenger craft.

"First reports of the incident gave the time of sighting the plane as Friday morning, but this was declared by Stuart to be in error as he saw the mysterious flyer at 11:30 o'clock Thursday night. The Coldwater location at the time was given as latitude 34:01 degrees north, longitude 68:08 degree west.

MYSTERIOUS AIRPLANE REPORTED BY SEAMEN

SAVANNAH, Ga., Sept. 2 (AP).—A vivid account of an unidentified airplane, sighted last Thursday night winging its way across the north Atlantic about 400 miles off the Virginia capes was given today upon arrival here of the steamship Coldwater, of the South Atlantic Steamship line.

Members of the crew told of the sighting of the plane, as related to them by Tom Stuart, third mate of the Coldwater, who was on watch at the time and was the only man aboard to see the adventurous flyer.

According to Stuart's report the plane was headed in the direction of Europe in the teeth of a gale which was sweeping along at a rate estimated by the ship's officers, at more than 100 miles an hour. Owing to the force of the gale it was impossible for Stuart to hear the engine, so he could not determine whether the plane was of the single or trimotored type. From the lights in the cabin, however, Stuart told the crew he gained the impression that it was a large passenger craft.

First reports of the incident gave the time of sighting the plane as Friday morning, but this was declared by Stuart to be in error as he saw the mysterious flyer at 11:30 o'clock Thursday night. The Coldwater's location at the time was given as latitude 34:01 degrees north, longitude 68:08 degrees west.

It was thought at first, members of the steamer's crew said, that the plane was en route to Bermuda, but Capt. A. C. Lindgren charted the flyer's course from the description given by Stuart and found that it lay well to the north of Bermuda.

An investigation of aeronautical experts failed to reveal any projected Atlantic and Bermuda flights and the opinion has been advanced that Stuart mistook some other sound of other ocean phenomena for an airplane.

*Chattanooga (Tenn.) Daily Times,
Sept. 3, 1929, p. 9*

"It was thought at first, members of the steamer crew said, that the plane was en route to Bermuda, but Capt. A. C. Lindgren charted the flyers course from the description given by Stuart and found that it lay well to the north of Bermuda.

"An investigation of aeronautical experts failed to reveal any projected Atlantic and Bermuda flights and the opinion has been advanced that Stuart mistook some other sound of other ocean phenomena for an airplane."

Since no airplane flights were supposed to be in the area, the object seen by Stuart remained unexplained. The object's high rate of speed, estimated at 100 miles per hour, and its immense size are very salient points, as is the fact that no sound was heard from the engines. This is a true UFO puzzle from the early 20th century.

43
THE UFO VISITORS
Spring Valley, New York
Summer 1929

HIGHLY RESPECTED New York UFO researcher Cheryl Costa, in a 2016 article titled "A 1929 Alien Abduction," disclosed an amazing UFO encounter from the Roaring Twenties. It was a case originally investigated by renowned alien abduction researcher Budd Hopkins (1931-2011). In her article, Costa points out that, although many people think alien abductions were not reported prior to the 1960s, a case of abduction is believed to have happened in 1929, making it one of the earliest known cases.

The incident occurred in the hamlet of Spring Valley in Rockland County, during the summer of

1929. The eyewitness, a 9-year-old girl, was playing outside her home when she noticed a flash of light from the sky above her.

Looking up, she saw what looked like a huge, metallic dirigible. All around the hull of the ship was a series of port holes or windows. The entire airship seemed to glow with an "unusual light."

Image by Matthias Wewering from Pixabay

What happened next was absolutely startling. The girl saw three or four humanoids, dressed in what looked like deep sea diving suits, coming out of the dirigible. The witness became aware that a number of animals all around the area had become strangely quiet and still.

The strange creatures seemed to "float" down to the ground, landing a short distance away from the eyewitness. Although scared, the girl was unable to move her feet or arms and thus could not escape.

Her next memory was of the creatures leaving her and floating back to their ship. She was not aware of how much time had passed since the UFO had first appeared.

Typical Deep Sea Diving Suit, 1913

When she returned home, her mother scolded her for being gone for "so long." It was then that she realized she was not able to remember everything that happened to her during her strange encounter with the humanoid creatures that had come from the mysterious airship.

As time passed, the girl developed a phobia about being alone and was perpetually haunted by nightmares about being chased by the humanoids from the airship. Her nightmares continued for many years. She also came down with a bizarre illness that doctors were unable to diagnose. Later, she told people that she thought she might have caught some type of strange disease from the humanoids that had approached her.

UFO investigators looking back at her case today are convinced that the symptoms she experienced are identical to those experienced by persons who claim they have been abducted by aliens. It's quite sad that she had to endure such a traumatic experience before abductees like Betty and Barney Hill and Travis Walton brought the phenomenon to the forefront of the public consciousness.

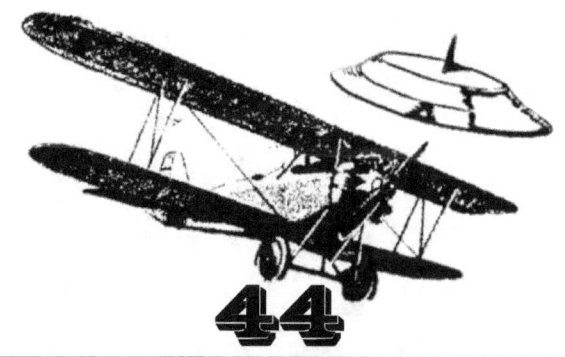

44

KNOCKED DOWN BY UFO

Oak Park, Illinois
September 1929

AS REPORTED IN Linda Zimmerman's excellent book *More Hudson Valley UFOs* (2017), a fascinating case of a close encounter with a UFO by a medical student named William Walton occurred in Oak Park, Illinois, in September of 1929.

Zimmerman located data on the incident in old case files from the Aerial Phenomena Research Organization (APRO), founded in 1952 by Jim and Coral Lorenzen, of Sturgeon Bay, Wisconsin.

*Oak Park, Illinois, in 1919. Shown is Oak Park
native Ernest Hemingway*

Walton's encounter began on a moonless, star-filled evening at 10:30 p.m. He was walking north on Euclid Avenue when he saw "a very bright yellowish-white diffused light; elliptically shaped like two saucers face to face."

The object appeared to be about 40 feet in diameter and about 2 feet in height. The UFO passed over Walton at an altitude of about 100 feet.

The object made a distinct humming sound "like turbines," and it emitted both heat and pressure down from above. The downward force emanating from the UFO caused Walton to fall to his knees.

It was moving north to south at high speed and then veered off to the southwest. The sighting lasted approximately 30 seconds.

After it had passed, the odor of sulfur was strong. Walton, although amazed and shaken, was not injured, and did not report the incident for fear of ridicule.

In her book, Zimmerman said, "This case stands out for a variety of reasons. First, the incident appears to have been experienced by an educated, reputable individual, involving a very early and close saucer sighting. Then there is the fact of this intense pressure, which actually knocked the man down to his knees! The strong smell of sulfur, while unusual, has been reported over the years in a number of cases. Add to all of this the heat and turbine-like humming noise, and this becomes a very special case that was seen, smelled, and felt."

In any case, the last recorded UFO sighting of the Roaring Twenties was literally a knockout!

Image by Patrick Fischer from Pixabay

INDEX

ABOUT THE AUTHOR

Noe Torres is a recognized expert in the field of UFOs and the paranormal. He is an author, publisher, and member of the Mutual UFO Network (MUFON). He holds a Bachelor's in English and a Master's in Library Science from the University of Texas at Austin. He has written one of the most popular books about the famous Roswell Incident, titled *Ultimate Guide to the Roswell UFO Crash*, which is the top selling book among tourists visiting Roswell, New Mexico. He has also written several other well-reviewed books, including *Mexico's Roswell*, *The Other Roswell*, *Aliens in the Forest*, *Fallen Angel*, and *The Coyame Incident*.

Noe has appeared on several nationally-broadcast television shows, including season 2, episode 1 of the Travel Channel's *Mysteries of the Outdoors*, titled "Strange Attraction," which premiered in August 2017. In that show, he is interviewed extensively about unexplained mysteries in Big Bend National Park. Also, in 2017, Noe was featured in an episode titled "The Marfa Lights" for the TV series *Mysteries of the Unexplained*. In 2008, he appeared in season 1, episode 4 of the

History Channel's *UFO Hunters*, in a show called "Crash and Retrieval."

Noe has appeared several times on George Noory's famous radio show *Coast to Coast AM*, as well as on The Jeff Rense Program and may other shows. He is also in high demand as a speaker at UFO and paranormal conferences and festivals, having been a featured speaker at the 2017 International UFO Congress in Scottsdale, Arizona. He has also spoken five times at the annual Roswell UFO Conference and at many other UFO conferences throughout the United States and Mexico.

ABOUT THE AUTHOR

John LeMay was born and raised in Roswell, NM, the "UFO Capital of the World." He is the author of over 30 books on film and western history such as *Kong Unmade: The Lost Films of Skull Island*, *Tall Tales and Half Truths of Billy the Kid*, and *Roswell USA: Towns That Celebrate UFOs, Lake Monsters, Bigfoot and Other Weirdness*. He is also the editor/publisher of *The Lost Films Fanzine* and has written for magazines such as *True West*, *Cinema Retro*, and *Mad Scientist* to name only a few. He is a Past President of the Board of Directors for the Historical Society for Southeast New Mexico.

ALSO AVAILABLE

CRYPTOZOOLOGY/COWBOYS & SAURIANS

Cowboys & Saurians: Prehistoric Beasts as Seen by the Pioneers explores dinosaur sightings from the pioneer period via real newspaper reports from the time. Well-known cases like the Tombstone Thunderbird are covered along with more obscure cases like the Crosswicks Monster and more. Softcover (357 pp/5.06" X 7.8") Suggested Retail: $19.95 ISBN: 978-1-7341546-1-0

Cowboys & Saurians: Ice Age zeroes in on snowbound saurians like the Cerato-saurus of the Arctic Circle and a Tyrannosaurus of the Tundra, as well as sightings of Ice Age megafauna like mammoths, glyptodonts, Sarkastodons and Saber-toothed tigers. Tales of a land that time forgot in the Arctic are also covered. Softcover (264 pp/5.06" X 7.8") Suggested Retail: $14.99 ISBN: 978-1-7341546-7-2

Southerners & Saurians takes the series formula of exploring newspaper accounts of monsters in the pioneer period with an eye to the Old South. In addition to dinosaurs are covered Lizardmen, Frogmen, giant leeches and mosquitoes, and the Dingocroc, which might be an alien rather than a prehistoric survivor. Softcover (202 pp/5.06" X 7.8") Suggested Retail: $13.99 ISBN: 978-1-7344730-4-9

Cowboys & Saurians South of the Border explores the saurians of Central and South America, like the Patagonian Plesiosaurus that was really an Iemisch, plus tales of the Neo-Mylodon, a menacing monster from underground called the Minhocao, Glyptodonts, and even Bolivia's three-headed dinosaur! Softcover (412 pp/ 5.06"X7.8") Suggested Retail: $17.95 ISBN: 978-1-953221-73-5

UFOLOGY/THE REAL COWBOYS & ALIENS IN CONJUNCTION WITH ROSWELL BOOKS

The Real Cowboys and Aliens: Early American UFOs explores UFO sightings in the USA between the years 1800-1864. Stories of encounters sometimes involved famous figures in U.S. history such as Lewis and Clark, and Thomas Jefferson.Hardcover (242pp/6" X 9") Softcover (262 pp/5.06" X 7.8") Suggested Retail: $24.99 (hc)/$15.95(sc) ISBN: 978-1-7341546-8-9\(hc)/978-1-7344 730-8-7(sc)

The second entry in the series, *Old West UFOs*, covers reports spanning the years 1865-1895. Includes tales of Men in Black, Reptilians, Spring-Heeled Jack, Sasquatch from space, and other alien beings, in addition to the UFOs and airships. Hardcover (276 pp/6" X 9") Softcover (308 pp/5.06" X 7.8") Suggested Retail: $29.95 (hc)/$17.95(sc) ISBN: 978-1-7344730-0-1 (hc)/ 978-1-73447 30-2-5 (sc)

The third entry in the series, *The Coming of the Airships*, encompasses a short time frame with an incredibly high concentration of airship sightings between 1896-1899. The famous Aurora, Texas, UFO crash of 1897 is covered in depth along with many others. Hardcover (196 pp/6" X 9") Softcover (222 pp/5.06" X 7.8") Suggested Retail: $24.99 (hc)/$15.95(sc) ISBN: 978-1-7347816 -1-8 (hc)/978-1-7347816-0-1(sc)

Early 20th Century UFOs kicks off a new series that investigates UFO sightings of the early 1900s. Includes tales of UFOs sighted over the *Titanic* as it sunk, Nikola Tesla receiving messages from the stars, an alien being found encased in ice, and a possible virus from outer space!Hardcover (196 pp/6" X 9") Softcover (222 pp/5.06" X 7.8") Suggested Retail: $27.99 (hc)/$16.95(sc) ISBN: 978-1-7347816-1-8 (hc)/978-1-73478 16-0-1(sc)